Embracing Our Call

Embracing Our Call
A Practical Guide for Church Governing Body Leaders

© 2025 Keith Clark-Hoyos
All rights reserved.

No part of this publication may be reproduced, stored in a retrieval system, or transmitted in any form or by any means—
electronic, mechanical, photocopying, recording, or otherwise—
without the prior written permission of the author,
except in the case of brief quotations embodied in critical articles or reviews.

Published by Clark-Hoyos Publishing
ISBN: 979-8-9987673-2-6

Library of Congress Control Number: [Pending]

Cover and interior design by Keith Clark-Hoyos

Printed in the United States of America

Scripture quotations are from the New Revised Standard Version Updated Edition (NRSVue), unless otherwise noted. Used by permission. All rights reserved.

This book is intended to support leaders across diverse Christian traditions. The content reflects shared practices in church governance and is not intended as legal, financial, or doctrinal advice. Always consult your denomination's policies and local regulations when implementing changes.

For bulk orders, permissions, or additional resources, please contact:
service@ChurchTrainingCenter.com

Embracing Our Call

A Practical Guide for Church Governing Body Leaders

Keith Clark-Hoyos

*To the faithful leaders
who serve not for recognition,
but for love of God and community.*

*And to every congregation
that dares to listen for the Spirit's call
and follow it together.*

Acknowledgments

Thank you to the churches for whom I have had the privilege to serve throughout my life; from an intern while in Bible College, to the churches in the Conference I served, to the churches I serve through Church Training Center. You have shaped me. You have challenged me. You have helped me develop my love letter to the Church!

To my beautiful wife, Zulima, who stands by my side in every act of service, every challenge of being a business owner, and in every celebration of a life or church transformed!

About the Author

Keith Clark-Hoyos is a dedicated leader known for his unwavering positivity and remarkable ability to guide and inspire within the realm of church leadership and administration. His life journey has been characterized by a deep commitment to personal and professional growth, a passion for teaching and coaching, and a profound love for nurturing individuals and organizations toward their highest potential.

In 2015, Keith transitioned from his role as a church judicatory leader to found Church Training Center — a thriving consulting, coaching, training, and accounting firm serving churches and nonprofits across the nation. Together with his wife and partner, he has built a team that supports mission-driven ministries with clarity, care, and Spirit-led wisdom.

Keith holds a Master of Arts in Ministry, Leadership & Service from Claremont School of Theology and an undergraduate degree in Business Administration and Church Ministries from Simpson University. He is also a Daoist Monk in the Wù Zhēn Pài (Awakened Reality Sect) lineage and brings a deeply contemplative and spiritually grounded presence to his work.

At the heart of Keith's calling is a desire to empower church leaders to live faithfully, lead effectively, and align all resources — financial, human, and spiritual — with the mission God has placed before them.

Table of Contents

Part One: Centering in God's Call

1. The Spirit Has Placed Us Here _____3
2. Paths Made Straight _____17
3. The Threefold Cord _____27
4. Stewarding the Storehouse _____37
5. Until the Sun Set _____47
6. Hearing the Silence _____59

Part Two: Structures That Support the Call

7. Wisdom That Builds the House _____75
8. Forming Our Structure _____85
9. Sealed in Covenant _____95
10. Meeting in the Presence of God _____103
11. Movement Leads to Stillness _____111

Part Three: Protecting What's Sacred

12. Shepherds After My Own Heart _____121
13. The Watchtower and the Shepherd _____129
14. Keeping the Wolves at Bay _____139
15. Accountability in Action _____149

16. Subjecting to Governing Authorities _____ 163

Part Four: Resourcing the Vision

17. Plans Committed in Prayer _____ 187
18. Written On Our Hearts- _____ 195
19. Compel People to Come In _____ 205
20. Bringing in the Harvest _____ 213
21. Leaving an Inheritance _____ 221
22. Threads to Refuse _____ 231

Part Five: Leading with Grace in Difficult Times

23. Blessed Are the Peacemakers _____ 239
24. Healed and Whole Again _____ 253
25. Iron Sharpens Iron _____ 263
26. When the Eye Rejects the Hand _____ 273
27. Unity in Calling _____ 281
Conclusion _____ 289
Appendix _____ i

Glossary of Governance & Finance Terms _____ ii
10 Practices of Spirit-Led Governance _____ iii
Scripture Index _____ v

Part One: Centering in God's Call

"And when you turn to the right or to the left, your ears will hear a voice behind you, saying, 'This is the way; walk in it.'"

– Isaiah 30:21

Part One: Centering in God's Call

This section serves as the spiritual and strategic foundation of the book, based on the Called Together discernment process. It explores why church governance matters, how to discern God's voice together, and how to align our collective life with the Spirit's direction.

- A Shared Call to Discernment
- The Way We Listen
- The Work of Alignment
- The Threefold Cord
- Stewards of the Church's Strength

Chapter 1:
The Spirit Has Placed Us Here

Rediscovering why we are here, together, and what Spirit-led governance truly means

"But now God has set the members, each one of them, in the body just as He pleased."

– 1 Corinthians 12:18

You are not here by accident.

You didn't stumble into leadership simply because someone needed a volunteer or you felt guilty saying no. You're not on the board or council because you have the right last name or the most free time or because you've always done it. You are here because the Spirit placed you here. And that matters more than you might realize.

Church governance is not just a necessary function of organized religion. It is a form of ministry. It is a space of discernment, stewardship, and sacred accountability. It is a spiritual practice—whether we've named it as such or not.

When the church treats governance like an administrative task instead of a spiritual responsibility, something begins to unravel. Decisions become reactive. Meetings become draining. Budgets become battlegrounds. And slowly, sometimes without noticing, we lose our way.

But when we begin with the recognition that God has called and placed us for a purpose—that changes everything.

This chapter is an invitation to remember that truth: you were placed here by the Spirit, not by accident but by intention. And the people around your table—whatever their strengths or weaknesses—were placed here too.

We don't always know why. We don't always feel worthy of it. We may not always agree with who's sitting beside us. But our job isn't to second-guess God's placement. Our job is to listen together for what the Spirit is doing in and through this particular gathering of people, in this particular season, in this particular church.

That's the beginning of Spirit-led governance.

It begins by asking, with humility and hope:

"Why has God gathered us now?"

"What is the Spirit doing in our midst?"

"What is ours to carry—and what isn't?"

In many churches, governing bodies spend most of their time reacting.

We react to financial strain. We react to conflict. We react to declining attendance or shifting community needs. We react to change—whether that change is coming from inside the church or the world around us.

But the work of governance was never meant to be reactive. It was meant to be discerning.

Discernment doesn't mean waiting until a crisis hits. Discernment is a continual posture of listening for the Spirit—especially when everything is going well, and especially when it isn't.

Discernment asks:

What is God inviting us to do or become right now?

Is this action aligned with the reason God has placed us here?

Are we spending our energy and resources on what matters most?

Without a clear and communal understanding of our Calling, we will drift.

Even faithful people will drift.

Even committed churches will drift.

We will begin to do things simply because we've always done them.

We will hold onto programs that no longer serve the congregation's needs.

We will pursue good ideas that may not be ours to pursue.

We don't drift because we're unfaithful.

We drift because we forget to anchor ourselves in discernment.

And the first anchor is this:

God has placed us here.

Not somewhere else. Not in another era. Not in another church. Here.

The Spirit has placed us in this moment.

And once we remember that—we can begin the sacred work of governance again.

That work is not about solving problems.

It's about tending the life of the church so that the church can live out its Calling in the world.

What does it mean to govern with Calling at the center?

It means that before we ask what's realistic, we ask what's faithful.

Before we assess what we can afford, we ask what we're being asked to become.

Before we plan next year's calendar, we pause to ask what season God has us in right now.

When Calling is clear, everything else begins to align:

Energy becomes focused instead of scattered.

Resources become tools of purpose instead of burdens of scarcity.

Meetings become spaces of clarity instead of tension.

But that doesn't happen automatically.

In most churches, governance energy tends to follow the loudest voice, the biggest crisis, or the path of least resistance. When that becomes the default, the governing body begins to feel:

Overwhelmed

Mistrusted

Confused

Burnt out

Why? Because the energy is being spent without a center.

We might be working hard—but not necessarily working faithfully.

We may be keeping the church functioning—but we're not aligning it with its Calling.

That's why the framework we use matters.

And in Spirit-led governance, that framework begins with four continual questions:

Calling – What is God inviting us to do or become?

Energy – How are we engaging with each other and with the work?

Resources – What has been entrusted to us, and how are we stewarding it?

Discernment – How are we listening for the Spirit's ongoing direction?

These questions are not just theological reflection points.

They are practical governance tools.

They help us check for alignment.

Because when Calling, Energy, and Resources are aligned, a church feels focused, empowered, and fruitful.

But when they are not—when our resources are used for things that are no longer aligned with our Calling, or our energy is consumed by unresolved tension—then ministry begins to fracture.

The church doesn't fall apart overnight. But it starts to feel heavy.

The board starts to feel tired.

The staff begins to feel unsupported.

And the members begin to disengage—not because they don't care, but because something feels off.

And they're right. Something is.

What's off is the alignment. And it can be restored.

Restoring alignment begins with Naming.

Not fixing. Not reacting. Not blaming.

Just naming.

Naming what God has already made clear.

Naming where we've strayed from the path—not in shame, but in truth.

Naming what the Spirit may be asking us to release.

And naming where we are being invited to begin again.

This is the work of the governing body.

It's not about being the most efficient team. It's about being the most faithful one.

And that means becoming a board that listens before it speaks.

That prays before it plans.

That gathers not just to get through an agenda, but to ask together, "What is God doing among us right now?"

That kind of leadership is not flashy.

It is not urgent.

It is not always visible from the outside.

But it is deep. And it is sustainable. And it is holy.

When churches live this way—when governing bodies become centers of discernment rather than centers of control—something shifts.

The congregation senses it.

The staff feels it.

The community experiences it.

Because a board aligned with the Spirit radiates peace.

Even in conflict.

Even in uncertainty.

Even in scarcity.

Why? Because they're not leading alone.

They're leading in response to something deeper.

To Someone deeper.

To the Spirit who placed them there.

One of the most common frustrations we hear from church leaders is this:

"It feels like I'm doing everything, and no one else is showing up."

Or…

"We have meetings, but nothing really changes."

Or even…

"We're stuck."

And often, the impulse is to try harder. To make more announcements. To host another training. To ask the same people to do just a little bit more.

But what if the answer isn't more?

What if the answer is alignment?

Because when your Calling is clear—and your Energy and Resources are aligned to that Calling—momentum returns. Not because you pushed harder, but because you stopped pushing in every direction at once.

Think of it like rowing a boat.

If each person on the team is rowing with strength, but in slightly different directions, you don't go anywhere. Or worse, you go in circles. But if everyone rows in the same direction—even with less strength—you move forward.

In Spirit-led governance, we don't row faster. We row together. We align our movements to the movement of the Spirit.

And to do that, we must ask:

Are we still centered in our Calling?

Is our board organized in a way that sustains life—not just structure?

Are our resources being used with intention, or just by habit?

Are we making decisions aligned with prayer—or just tradition?

This isn't about judgment. It's about attention.

It's about paying attention to the places where we are out of sync with the Spirit—and gently, courageously, realigning ourselves to God's invitation.

Sometimes, that means letting go of what no longer fits.

Sometimes, it means saying no to something that sounds good but isn't ours to carry.

And sometimes, it means resting, so that the next step can emerge in silence.

There will always be more to do.

There will always be concerns about finances, volunteers, aging buildings, denominational expectations, cultural shifts. The list doesn't end.

But your role as a governing body is not to carry all of it alone.

Your role is to listen. To discern. To be faithful to the piece of God's work that has been entrusted to you.

This chapter began with a simple truth:

The Spirit has placed you here.

Let that truth anchor you.

Let it soften your fear when the path ahead feels unclear.

Let it quiet the inner pressure to fix everything right away.

Let it remind you that you are not leading alone.

You are not here because you're the most qualified.

You're here because you were called.

You're here because God is doing something in your church—and you've been entrusted with the sacred work of tending that unfolding.

So breathe.

Return to that truth often.

Let it shape your meetings.

Let it guide your questions.

Let it interrupt your assumptions.

Let it create space for silence.

Let it lead you into alignment with the Spirit—not just strategy.

And when you feel lost or overwhelmed or unsure, return again to this:

"But now God has set the members, each one of them, in the body just as He pleased."

God has placed you here.

Not randomly. Not casually.

But lovingly. Purposefully. Spiritually.

Your leadership matters—not because you're in control, but because you are willing to listen.

And listening is the first act of faithful governance.

You've said yes to something holy.

And this book? It's not just a guide—it's a companion.

We'll walk through alignment, discernment, sacred structure, and the courage it takes to lead when the way is not clear.

You won't be given formulas.

You'll be invited into rhythm.

You won't be handed answers.

You'll be offered practices to listen for the Spirit together.

What lies ahead is practical.

But it's also deeply spiritual.

Because governance is not just about what we decide.

It's about who we become as we listen for God's call—and respond with integrity, courage, and care.

Let's begin.

Closing Image

Imagine a table in a quiet room. The chairs are mismatched. The light flickers softly. Around that table sit people who didn't choose each other—but were chosen. Not by coincidence. Not by convenience. But by the Spirit. You sit among them not as a strategist, not as a volunteer filling a gap, but as one entrusted with a sacred moment. You may not know all that lies ahead. But this much is true: you are here. And the Spirit is, too.

❦ Discernment Questions

- What evidence do we see that God has placed us together for a purpose?
- In what ways have we drifted from our calling as a church?
- Where do we need to pause and listen more deeply for the Spirit's direction?
- Are our current resources (time, energy, money) aligned with what we believe God is calling us to do?
- What do we need to release in order to follow where God is leading now?

Chapter 2:

Paths Made Straight

The importance of aligning Calling, Energy, and Resources to avoid confusion and strife

"Trust in the Lord with all your heart and lean not on your own understanding; in all your ways submit to him, and he will make your paths straight."

– Proverbs 3:5–6

"Trust in the Lord with all your heart and lean not on your own understanding; in all your ways submit to him, and he will make your paths straight."

Church boards rarely begin in chaos. Most are composed of thoughtful, prayerful people doing their best. But even when everyone is sincere, something can slowly shift. Momentum slows. Meetings circle the same topics. Energy feels scattered. Vision clouds. You may sense that something is "off"—not broken, not hostile, just… out of sync. This chapter is about recognizing that subtle shift, and learning to respond before disconnection becomes dysfunction. In Chapter 1, we remembered that our placement on the governing body is not accidental. We were called. And our shared calling forms the foundation for Spirit-led governance. But having a shared calling isn't enough. Just as a house needs both a foundation and a frame, governance needs both clarity of purpose and alignment in practice. That's what makes the path straight. Not easier. Not frictionless. But faithful. Alignment doesn't mean everyone agrees on every decision. It means that the decisions, the discussions, the strategies, and the spending all flow from a shared sense of what God is inviting this congregation to be and do. When that alignment is strong, churches can face hardship with peace. When it's weak, even simple conversations can turn into confusion.

Think of a church board not as a set of individuals, but as one body. That body needs to move with cohesion. If one part is sprinting while another is dragging, if one part is focused on preservation while another is pushing for reinvention, the result is spiritual whiplash. It's not that anyone is wrong. It's that no one is moving together. That's what misalignment feels like. And it can show up in subtle, familiar ways.

Misalignment is not a moral failure. It's not the result of a lack of faith or effort. It's a natural consequence of movement without shared direction. And it can happen quietly—especially in seasons of transition, growth, or fatigue. Sometimes a church board starts to say "yes" to too many things. Sometimes one or two passionate leaders carry the energy while the rest of the team struggles to keep up. Sometimes the budget gets reused year after year with only minor edits, no longer reflecting what God is currently calling the church to pursue. These are all signs that something is out of alignment.

In our work with churches, we often hear familiar patterns. A board is exhausted. A pastor feels isolated. A congregation seems disengaged. But underneath those feelings, there's often a deeper cause: the church is spending energy and resources in ways that no longer reflect its current calling. It's not that people are unwilling—it's that the direction has become unclear. When there is no shared discernment, good intentions pull in competing directions. Committees make plans without coordination. Money gets allocated based on habit, not purpose. Ministries run parallel instead of together. And the board, rather than being a center of clarity, becomes a place of reaction.

That's why alignment matters. Alignment is not rigidity. It's not forcing everyone into agreement or eliminating creative differences. Alignment is when each piece of the church's governance—its decisions, its finances, its leadership energy—moves in the same direction: toward the calling God has placed on the congregation now. Not last year. Not twenty years ago. Now.

Let's look more closely at five common signs that a board has drifted out of alignment. These are not accusations—they're invitations. Invitations to pause, to reflect, and to return to center.

1. **The board is unclear about its role.** Meetings shift toward operational micromanagement or disengaged rubber-stamping. Members feel uncertain about whether they're offering leadership or just managing tasks. This often happens when there's no shared sense of what the board is uniquely responsible for protecting or guiding.
2. **Decisions feel inconsistent.** One issue is handled with urgency, the next with indifference. Policies are unclear or unevenly applied. The board responds to personalities or

circumstances instead of discerned direction. Without guiding principles, leadership becomes reactive.
3. **Energy is high—but scattered.** Passionate people bring ideas, but there's no filter for determining what fits the church's calling. Everything sounds good, but not everything belongs. Volunteers feel stretched thin. The pastor is overextended. The board is busy—but not necessarily effective.
4. **Budget conversations are tense and disconnected.** Money feels like a source of anxiety instead of a tool for ministry. The board debates line items but avoids asking whether the spending reflects what God is actually calling the church to do. Without that connection, finances become about survival, not stewardship.
5. **Spiritual reflection is missing.** Meetings are full of reports and decisions, but short on silence, prayer, or discernment. The Spirit is invoked in opening prayers but rarely consulted in conversation. Over time, governance becomes more about tasks than transformation.

Each of these signs is a signal, not a sentence. They don't mean a board has failed. They mean it's time to pause, recalibrate, and realign.

Realignment begins with a pause. Not a retreat from responsibility, but a moment of holy attention. Before adopting a new strategy or approving next year's budget, a faithful board asks: Are we centered in our Calling? Are our Resources directed toward what matters most? Is our Energy being used wisely—or just used up?

This pause is not passive. It's one of the most powerful spiritual practices a governing body can undertake. In the pause, we notice what we've been carrying. We ask what can be set down. We listen for what the Spirit might be calling us toward next.

Sometimes the answers come quickly. Sometimes they emerge slowly, in silence or shared prayer. Either way, the act of pausing clears space for discernment. And from that space, decisions come with greater clarity, integrity, and peace.

Take, for example, a congregation struggling with a beautiful, aging building. The cost of upkeep is steadily rising. A few members suggest launching a capital campaign, while others want to rent the space to external groups. At the same time, the church's food ministry is growing—and running out of space. Meetings get heated. The board feels stuck. But when they pause to ask, "What is God calling us to do with our building?", a different conversation begins. They realize the goal isn't to preserve a building—it's to create space for ministry. From that clarity, a new idea emerges: convert part of the sanctuary into a weekday café that supports the food ministry. The space becomes mission-aligned, not just historically maintained.

Or consider the board that approves every idea because they're eager to say yes to passion. A new book study? Yes. A community garden? Yes. A podcast? Sure. The list grows, and so does the burnout. No one's quite sure how all the pieces fit. Energy is everywhere—but the impact is fuzzy. When this board finally pauses to reflect, they realize they never stopped to ask which of these ideas actually aligned with their current season and capacity. Through prayer and conversation, they recommit to two initiatives that support their core calling—and put the rest on hold, not as rejection, but as discernment.

Then there's the finance committee that reviews every line item for accuracy but struggles to connect the numbers to ministry. Meetings focus on dollars, not stories. Questions arise like: "Why are we still funding this?" "What does this expense even do?" Frustration builds. But after a realignment conversation, the board begins a new rhythm: for each major line item, they share one recent story of ministry impact. Suddenly, numbers come to life. The conversation shifts from protection to purpose.

Realignment is not just about fixing. It's about re-centering. And that practice can become a rhythm. Some boards now begin every meeting with five minutes of silence, asking: "Where have we strayed from our shared calling this month?" Others commit to quarterly retreats for listening, not planning. Still others use a simple set of alignment questions at the top of every agenda to frame their work.

Realignment does not always require sweeping change. Sometimes, it simply asks for clarity. Clarity about what to say yes to—and what to release. Clarity about what matters most right now—not five years ago. Clarity about how God is shaping your congregation's future, one faithful decision at a time.

When alignment returns, the atmosphere shifts. Meetings gain purpose. Communication becomes clearer. Conflict loses its edge. Discernment becomes a shared practice rather than an individual burden. The church starts to feel like it's moving forward—not just functioning, but flourishing.

And perhaps most importantly, people begin to trust the process again. Because when Calling, Energy, and Resources move in harmony, the governing body becomes what it was meant to be: a place of clarity, courage, and spiritual leadership.

That doesn't mean it will always be smooth. Faithful paths still include hills, turns, and unknowns. But they are straight in the sense that they are true. True to what God is doing in your midst. True to what the Spirit is whispering. True to the purpose for which you were gathered.

So take the time to notice. To listen. To realign.

Because alignment isn't a destination. It's a spiritual rhythm. One that allows a board to move together, not in perfection—but in faith.

Closing Image

Picture a worn trail through a dense forest. It's not paved. It twists. It rises and dips. But it's clear. Someone walked this before you. Someone marked the way. When the clouds gather or the path narrows, you do not panic—you pause. You remember who you are and why you started. And then you walk again. Not with certainty in every step, but with trust in the direction. That is what alignment feels like. Not perfection. But peace.

🕊 Discernment Questions

- Where do we sense tension, fatigue, or confusion in our governance life?
- Are we managing the church—or discerning what God is asking of us right now?
- What energy are we spending that doesn't feel connected to our current Calling?
- What practices could help us pause and listen more deeply in our meetings?
- If we made one change this month to bring greater alignment, what would it be?

Chapter 3:
The Threefold Cord

Building unity and strength through spiritual, relational, and organizational alignment.

"Though one may be overpowered, two can defend themselves. A cord of three strands is not quickly broken."

– Ecclesiastes 4:12

"For where two or three are gathered in my name, I am there among them."

– Matthew 18:20

"Above all, clothe yourselves with love, which binds everything together in perfect harmony."

– Colossians 3:14

"Though one may be overpowered, two can defend themselves. A cord of three strands is not quickly broken."

Some churches operate like machines. Others, like families. Some lean heavily into strategy, while others emphasize spirit. But the most faithful, resilient, and Spirit-led congregations hold a sacred tension: they are both relational and structured, both prayerful and practical. When these dimensions are in harmony, ministry flows. When they're not, things fray — often invisibly at first.

This chapter is about the strength that comes from weaving together three essential strands of healthy church life: Spiritual Unity – shared Calling and devotion to God's ongoing movement. Relational Trust – mutual respect, compassion, and honesty in leadership. Organizational Clarity – clear roles, structures, and expectations that support the work. Each of these is valuable on its own. But only when braided together do they create something durable — a cord that can withstand pressure, conflict, or fatigue.

One Strand Alone Can Be Snapped

When a church board is grounded only in spiritual intention without relational or structural support, it risks becoming idealistic but ineffective. Meetings begin with prayer, but quickly drift. Everyone wants to listen to the Spirit, but no one knows who's responsible for what. Decisions are made loosely or never finalized. Frustration builds quietly because there's no healthy channel for processing tension. People burn out — not because they lack faith, but because there's no container for the fire.

When a board prioritizes relationship but avoids clarity, it can become conflict-averse and emotionally entangled. People are hesitant to name problems because they don't want to hurt feelings. Responsibilities are fuzzy. Expectations are assumed rather than articulated. Those who speak truth might feel like they're "causing drama," while those who withdraw may be silently shouldering too much. In the name of kindness, clarity gets lost — and with it, accountability.

When a board emphasizes structure without nurturing spiritual or relational life, it can become rigid and cold. Meetings are efficient but shallow. Decisions are processed quickly, but often disconnected from prayer or discernment. Rules become tools for control rather than containers for purpose. People feel like they're just a cog in the machine — not a beloved member of Christ's body. Structure without soul doesn't lead a church. It just maintains an organization.

Braided Together, They Create Strength

When spiritual unity, relational trust, and organizational clarity are aligned, something sacred emerges. The board trusts each other enough to name hard truths. The structure is clear enough to distribute work fairly. The Spirit is honored enough to interrupt or redirect any of it. And when that happens, the whole community begins to experience: Less confusion. More joy in leadership. Greater resilience in hard seasons. A culture of discernment, not just management.

Sometimes, churches don't realize the cord is unraveling until something snaps. A decision is made that bypasses the board entirely. The pastor feels isolated. Longtime members stop attending meetings. A conflict emerges that no one knows how to address. Or… nothing dramatic happens at all — just slow disconnection, creeping fatigue, and the silent erosion of trust. None of this usually starts with bad intent. It starts when one strand is overused and the others are neglected.

Common Signs of an Unraveled Cord

1. Over-Spiritualizing Without Structure: Every issue is deferred to prayer, but decisions linger unresolved. Discernment becomes a way to delay, rather than a call to act. Conflict is avoided because "we should all just be gracious." There's little accountability — only goodwill and hope.

2. Over-Structuring Without Relationship: Power dynamics creep in. People follow the rules but stop bringing their hearts to the table. The letter of the law becomes more important than the life of the church. Those with institutional memory feel displaced; newer leaders feel unseen.

3. Over-Relating Without Shared Calling: Meetings prioritize harmony over mission. Hard decisions are avoided to keep the peace. Leadership becomes personality-dependent — "We trust her," "We get along," "Let's not stir the pot." Vision becomes blurry because no one wants to disrupt relationships.

Each of these scenarios creates drift. And that drift can cost a church not just members or money — but vitality.

How Do We Begin to Reweave the Cord?

We begin by naming. Not blaming. Not fixing. Not overhauling. Just naming. Ask: Are we grounded in shared spiritual purpose right now? Do we trust one another enough to speak truthfully and kindly? Is our structure helping or hindering our ability to move forward together? These are not evaluation questions. They're realignment questions. They assume God is still moving, the Spirit is still speaking, and the board is still capable of weaving together a faithful response.

Restoring the Balance

Sometimes, one strand needs to be pulled forward intentionally for a season: If structure is too rigid: Lean into relationship and spiritual openness. Let the board slow down. Host a retreat. Reconnect. If relationships are frayed: Clarify responsibilities. Review your covenants. Recommit to communication norms. If purpose feels lost: Revisit your discerned Calling. Pause the projects. Ask again: What is God asking of us now? Faithful leadership isn't about balance in every meeting. It's about staying braided across time.

When the board practices weaving these three strands consistently, people begin to show up with more energy — because they're seen, supported, and spiritually grounded. No one person has to hold it all. The strength comes from the braid.

Practices that Strengthen the Cord

Healthy boards are not born — they're cultivated. And the cultivation happens in small, intentional practices that braid spiritual unity, relational trust, and organizational clarity into the very rhythm of governance.

1. Begin Every Meeting with Centering Prayer: More than a nod to faith, it's a way of remembering that God's presence is not theoretical — it's active, personal, and here.

2. Check in — Not Just In Attendance, But in Spirit: Before diving into reports and motions, pause to ask: How are we arriving today? What energy are we bringing? Where do we feel most connected — or disconnected — from our work?

3. Clarify Roles, Revisit Expectations: Every board needs periodic recalibration. When responsibilities go undefined, burnout and resentment follow. At least once a year, revisit role descriptions, communication norms, and decision-making pathways.

4. Reflect on Alignment at the End of Each Meeting: Close with a single question: Are we still woven together? Did this meeting reflect our shared Calling? Were our conversations grounded in trust and respect?

5. Normalize Repair: Even the strongest boards unravel sometimes. Apologize when needed. Name disconnection early. Return to spiritual grounding before pressing forward.

When Conflict Tests the Cord

Consider a small congregation where two long-serving leaders disagree about the future of worship style...Conflict will always arise. But when spiritual unity, relational trust, and organizational clarity are practiced regularly, boards are more resilient. They recover faster. They repair better. They return to their Calling more quickly. The cord holds.

Practice: Annual Covenant Renewal

One way to keep the threefold cord strong is by holding an annual covenant renewal session...Revisiting these questions fosters trust. It reminds people that governance is not static—it grows with the people who hold it.

Preparing to Sustain the Call

The strength of a threefold cord is not just for internal peace. It prepares the church to sustain its Calling over time...Because when governance becomes woven, not fractured, the church can carry more—and carry it faithfully.

Closing Image
Imagine holding a rope in your hands — thick, weathered, familiar. You know the strength of it not because it's unbreakable, but because it has held you through seasons of pull and pressure. This is what your leadership can be. Not perfect. Not effortless. But woven. Woven by Spirit. Woven by shared commitment. Woven by the sacred strength that comes from binding together in love.

A cord of three strands is not easily broken. So it is with governance grounded in spiritual alignment, relational trust, and organizational clarity. These three elements—each powerful on its own—find their greatest strength when woven together with intention and grace.

🕊 Discernment Questions

- Which part of the cord—spiritual, relational, or organizational—needs strengthening in our board right now?

- How are we cultivating trust among leaders beyond task-based roles?

- In what ways does our current structure help or hinder our spiritual unity?

- What practices could help us deepen alignment before making decisions?

- Are we confusing agreement with alignment, or do we have true shared discernment?

Chapter 4
Stewarding the Storehouse

Faithfully managing the time, talent, and treasure entrusted to the church for its Calling

"Each of you should use whatever gift you have received to serve others, as faithful stewards of God's grace in its various forms."
– 1 Peter 4:10

Every resource the church holds—every dollar, every hour volunteered, every skill offered—is a gift. Not earned. Not owned. Entrusted. Stewardship begins with this recognition. Our role as leaders is not to preserve what we have out of fear, nor to spend it aimlessly in pursuit of activity. Our role is to steward these gifts with reverence and clarity, so that they are used faithfully in alignment with the Calling God has placed upon our congregation.

In too many churches, stewardship is reduced to fundraising or financial reporting. But true stewardship is far more sacred. It is the practice of honoring what has been entrusted to us. That includes the money in the budget, yes—but it also includes the people serving in ministry, the attention we give to their capacity and well-being, the integrity of our systems, and the story we tell through every financial decision we make.

When we talk about "the storehouse," we are not speaking of a vault or a savings account. We are speaking of everything that sustains the church's mission—its time, its talent, its treasure, and its testimony. The storehouse holds not only the financial tools of ministry but the unseen strength of faith-filled leadership. Our work as a governing body is to protect that storehouse—not for our own comfort, but for the sake of the Calling it serves.

Faithful stewardship means more than keeping track of resources. It means aligning those resources to the mission. A church may have an accurate budget, clean books, and timely reports—but if those tools aren't shaped by Calling, they become just another task. The question is not only, "Are we managing funds well?" but "Are we using what's been entrusted to us in service of what God is asking us to do right now?"

This is where spiritual governance meets financial systems. A board grounded in Calling will not simply ask, "Can we afford this?" but "Does this reflect who we are called to be?" Budgets become not just spreadsheets, but statements of discernment. Policies become not just rules, but rhythms of protection. Reports become not just numbers, but narratives of ministry. What you track tells your story. What you protect reveals your priorities.

When boards begin from fear—fear of not having enough, fear of upsetting donors, fear of financial scrutiny—they risk drifting into either scarcity or secrecy. But when boards begin from Calling, stewardship becomes a form of worship. It honors the gifts of the congregation and tells the truth about what matters most. That truth requires both spiritual listening and practical structure.

This is why we emphasize systems that work—not systems that impress, but systems that serve. Systems grounded in GAAP principles, segregation of duties, transparent reporting, and written policies not only protect your resources—they protect your people. They reduce risk. They build trust. They tell your volunteers, staff, and donors: We take this seriously. We treat this as sacred.

It is a dangerous myth that financial controls communicate distrust. In truth, they communicate integrity. As one workshop participant once said, "I thought requiring two signatures meant we didn't trust each other. But now I see—it's because we do." Good systems don't restrict generosity. They protect it. They don't hinder ministry. They sustain it.

Too many churches have suffered from vague roles, missing documentation, or unspoken exceptions. We've heard the stories. Blank checks signed "just in case." Treasurers working in isolation with no regular review. Committees approving expenses with no written guidelines. These practices don't just invite risk—they erode trust in leadership, especially when mistakes or misconduct arise. When policies are unclear, enforcement feels personal. When policies are clear, accountability becomes shared.

As stewards, we must protect not only the money, but the relationships behind it. A well-crafted financial policy is a gift to your community. It helps new leaders step in without confusion. It offers transparency when questions arise. It ensures that no one is carrying too much alone. The burden of stewardship must be shared, just as the blessings of ministry are shared.

That's why systems matter. A trustworthy system includes policies for how funds are authorized, how checks are signed, how records are kept, and how reports are reviewed. It includes clarity about who approves what and how decisions are documented. It includes procedures for reconciling bank statements and reviewing income streams. These are not bureaucratic boxes to check. They are the unseen scaffolding that keeps the storehouse standing.

But stewardship is not just about control. It's also about communication. A budget is more than a ledger—it's a story. And the way we present that story shapes the response of the congregation. Too often, churches default to numbers without meaning. Line items without context. Charts without connection.

Instead, we are called to tell the truth about what we do that matters. To highlight ministry, not maintenance. To show how our collective offerings—time, talent, and treasure—are being transformed into worship, learning, outreach, and care. This is the heart of mission-oriented budgeting. It is not about justifying expenses. It is about witnessing to God's work among us.

When the congregation sees a pie chart, they should also see a people-fed, a child-nurtured, a neighbor-welcomed. They should hear stories—of the retreat that renewed a pastor, the retreat meal that comforted a grieving widow, the youth trip that transformed a teenager's faith. These are not embellishments. They are the reason the budget exists.

Clear, transparent, and mission-aligned communication builds generosity. It removes suspicion. It invites deeper investment. And it models the very stewardship we hope to see in others. If we expect the congregation to give with trust and joy, we must handle their gifts with clarity and care.

This is why we say: trust the system, not just the people. When your systems are strong, volunteers can lead with freedom. Treasurers can rest knowing they are supported. Pastors can focus on their Calling without fear of scandal or misunderstanding. And your church can move forward—not with anxiety, but with confidence.

There's a sacred rhythm to stewardship that gets lost when we rush. Some churches operate with urgency—scrambling to meet payroll, making last-minute decisions, or overextending because they "don't want to say no." Others become overly cautious—holding back funds out of fear, saying no reflexively, or defaulting to "what we've always done." Neither approach reflects faithfulness. Both are signs of misalignment.

Faithful stewardship asks: Are we moving at the pace of prayer? Are we making decisions rooted in Calling, not just pressure? Are we stewarding energy and resources in ways that renew life, not drain it?

This rhythm includes recognizing the seasons of financial life.

Every church has patterns—times of increase and times of tightening. A congregation might receive its largest offerings in December but struggle in the summer. Planning for these cycles isn't a lack of faith. It's a form of wisdom. Monitoring cash flow, building reserves, and reviewing five-year trends are all ways we keep the lamp burning. They let us plan for ministry from a place of steadiness rather than stress.

And when the season changes—when giving decreases or a new need arises—faithful boards don't panic. They pause. They pray. They listen. They reassess the alignment between Calling, Energy, and Resources. Sometimes the answer is to cut back. Sometimes the answer is to step forward in trust. But either way, the decision is made from discernment—not fear.

This is what makes stewardship different from fundraising. Fundraising asks, "How do we get more?" Stewardship asks, "How are we honoring what we've been given?" One is transactional. The other is transformational.

To be a steward of the storehouse is not simply to keep track of funds—it is to guard the sacred trust of the congregation. Every board member, every treasurer, every pastor shares in that responsibility. Together, you form the circle of care around God's resources. And that care is not neutral—it's formational. The way you handle church finances teaches others how to think about money. It shapes how your congregation sees generosity, transparency, and trust.

When your systems are clear, when your reporting is honest, when your policies are followed and your practices are grounded in purpose, you are not just doing administrative work—you are leading spiritually. You are modeling what it looks like to handle

God's gifts with reverence. You are saying, through your actions: "This matters. We honor what we have been given. We will not waste it. We will not hide it. We will use it well."

This is why financial reporting should never feel like an afterthought. It should be a testimony. Not just to the numbers—but to the movement of the Spirit. Use reports to celebrate what ministry was made possible. Use budget season to remind the church of who you are and what you're called to do. Use stewardship campaigns to tell stories of transformation, not just to meet goals.

And when the church sees the connection—between dollars and discipleship, between gifts and growth, between policies and purpose—the culture begins to shift. Stewardship becomes more than a financial task. It becomes a spiritual witness.

As we move into the next chapters—into structures, policies, and accountability—you'll see that none of it stands alone. Everything that follows exists to support this very truth: that governance is a sacred act of stewardship. The policies are meant to protect the people. The procedures are meant to preserve the witness. The structures are meant to sustain the Calling. Because in every decision, you are tending the storehouse—not to fill it with pride, but to open it with trust.

Closing Image

Imagine a quiet room lit by a single oil lamp. That lamp has burned through storms, through silence, through song. It didn't burn because someone demanded it to. It burned because someone tended it—quietly, faithfully, again and again. That's what stewardship is. It's not flashy. It's not about applause. It's about keeping the lamp lit so that others may see, may find shelter, may be reminded that the fire of Calling still burns within the heart of the church.

🪶 Discernment Questions

- Are our financial practices shaped more by habit or by Calling?

- In what ways are we protecting our people—not just our money—through clear policies and shared responsibility?

- What story are we telling through our budget? Does it reflect what we believe God is doing in our midst?

- Where are we experiencing anxiety around resources? What would it look like to respond with trust and clarity?

- What step can we take this season to strengthen the systems that hold our storehouse?

Chapter 5
Until the Sun Set

Discerning when the Calling is beyond your current means, and how to seek partnerships in peace

"When Moses' hands grew tired, they took a stone and put it under him and he sat on it. Aaron and Hur held his hands up—one on one side, one on the other—so that his hands remained steady till sunset."

– Exodus 17:12

Every church — no matter how faithful, committed, or Spirit-led — eventually arrives at a moment when it must say the words many leaders fear:

"We cannot do this alone."

This moment doesn't mean the church has failed. It doesn't mean the board has mismanaged. It doesn't mean the Calling was misheard.

It means this: the Calling is bigger than the capacity available right now.

This is sacred truth — and it is difficult to name. Because we live in a culture, and often serve in a church, that rewards self-sufficiency. Many governing bodies are conditioned to believe that asking for help is a sign of weakness. That real leaders "figure it out." That faithfulness means pushing through at all costs.

But Exodus 17 tells a different story.

Moses had led faithfully. He had heard God's voice. He had stepped into the hard work of leadership. But on that mountain — arms lifted, body trembling — he reached his limit.

And God didn't respond with judgment. God responded with Aaron and Hur.

They brought a stone for Moses to sit on. They stood beside him. They held his arms up.

Until the sun set.

This story is not about Moses' weakness. It is about shared strength.

And this is where many church boards miss the invitation.

They either push harder — trying to carry the weight themselves, adding more meetings, more expectations, more late nights. Or they pull back — scaling down, retreating, or quietly letting go of ministries that once brought life.

But there is a third way.

It is the way of honest discernment, rooted not in guilt or pride, but in trust.

Trust that the Spirit still provides. Trust that provision sometimes comes through people not yet at the table. Trust that partnership is not defeat — it is faith in motion.

Church boards often wait too long to name the strain.

Not out of negligence, but out of habit. Out of love. Out of a quiet, noble belief that "we should be able to handle this."

But strain has a way of building — slowly, silently — until the cracks begin to show. Not always in obvious ways. Sometimes it sounds like…

"I just don't have the energy I used to." "Let's put that decision off again." "We're stretched so thin, we can't even think about anything new."

Other times, it looks like:

The same people cycling through every leadership role. Meetings that go quiet when new ideas are proposed. Programs held together by last-minute stress and silent resentment. Budgets that reflect survival, not purpose. Volunteers who show up, but no longer with joy.

These are not signs of failure. They are signs of friction — when energy and Calling are out of sync.

And the longer the friction is ignored, the more likely it is to burn through what once felt sustainable.

What begins as strain becomes discouragement. Discouragement becomes disengagement. And soon, ministry becomes something to survive — not something that gives life.

This is where wise boards learn to listen with spiritual ears, not just strategic ones.

The question is not: "Can we make this work?" The real question is: "Is the Spirit asking us to carry this alone?"

Faithfulness isn't always found in holding on. Sometimes it's found in letting others hold part of the weight.

And this requires honesty.

It takes courage for a board to say: "We don't have the energy to do this well." "Our leadership structure isn't strong enough to carry this vision alone." "We need help — not eventually, but now."

Too often, churches confuse capacity with Calling. They assume if they can't do it all themselves, they must not have heard God correctly.

But some visions are intentionally given beyond the means of a single church.

Because God intends for the work to be shared.

This is not a flaw in the system. This is the design of the body of Christ.

Faithfulness in leadership is not about doing everything alone. It's about carrying what is yours to carry — and releasing what is not.

Many boards resist asking for help because they fear it signals failure. But in Scripture, asking for help is often the beginning of transformation.

In the early church, when needs outgrew the apostles' ability to serve, they named the strain and appointed new leaders (Acts 6). When Paul encountered churches in crisis or transition, he called on others to strengthen and support them. Even Jesus, in the garden, asked his disciples to stay and pray — and felt the sting of their absence when they didn't.

God has never required leaders to be superhuman. God has only asked them to be faithful.

And faithfulness includes partnership.

So what does that look like in the life of your church?

It could mean: Co-leading a ministry with another congregation.

Asking the judicatory for help with a pastoral transition. Applying for a grant that funds what your budget can't. Inviting a younger leader into a shared role — even if they aren't "ready" by old definitions. Hiring part-time staff where you once relied solely on volunteers. Letting go of one program in order to do another with excellence.

These are not signs of decline. They are signs of discernment.

As the Role of the Church Board Chair materials remind us, a strong board does not simply protect the status quo — it creates a leadership environment where truth can be spoken and support can be sought.

But seeking support requires a shift in mindset:

From scarcity to possibility. From isolation to interdependence. From doing more with less to doing what matters — with others.

When this shift happens, things begin to open: Meetings become less reactive. Visioning becomes less overwhelming. Ministry feels more alive, because it's no longer being carried by just a few.

Sometimes partnership doesn't mean funding or formal alliances. Sometimes it means creating internal partnerships — between teams, generations, or even within the board itself.

You might ask: "Who else can hold this with me?" "What part of this work can be shared or released?" "What strengths are in the room that haven't been named yet?" "Is this something we're meant to do — or something we're meant to bless others to do?"

These questions are not signs of confusion. They are signs of maturity.

Boards that regularly revisit these questions — and act on what they hear — often find that the energy they thought was gone returns in new form.

Not because the load is lighter. But because it is shared.

The image in Exodus 17 is not just about a single moment of support. It is about sustained faithfulness — even when energy runs low.

Moses didn't ask for help. But Aaron and Hur saw his fatigue and responded with grace. They didn't take over the work. They didn't walk away. They came alongside — and held his arms up.

That is partnership.

And that is what many churches need today.

Not just strategic plans. Not just financial infusions. But people and partners who are willing to say: "We'll hold this with you — until the sun sets."

This doesn't mean we avoid difficult decisions. It means we make them together, with clarity and compassion.

Sometimes, "holding each other up" means: Sharing the weight of hard conversations. Rotating leadership responsibilities. Creating space for sabbatical or rest. Inviting outside facilitators to help when the internal dynamics are too complex. Being willing to speak what others are only whispering.

In Creating a Healthy Church Governance Culture, we're reminded that churches thrive when their culture allows both honesty and hope. When people are trusted not only to serve, but to struggle out loud. When boards name exhaustion — not as failure, but as feedback from the body.

You are not less faithful when you are tired.

You are not less called when you say, "We need more hands. We need a stone to sit on."

You are not betraying the mission when you pause, step back, and ask what's sustainable.

Because the goal isn't to be heroic. The goal is to be steadily faithful — as long as the sun shines on what God has asked you to do.

And sometimes that means: Saying no to something beautiful because it's no longer yours to carry. Delaying a launch because the core team needs strengthening. Naming that a building project, a new hire, or a bold new vision is not possible alone.

This doesn't mean giving up.

It means giving the Spirit room to bring the right people to the table. The right partner. The right volunteer. The right funder. The right reframe.

One of the most courageous things a board can do is stop pretending they are limitless.

The people of Israel didn't win the battle because Moses was strong. They won because his strength was surrounded.

Your church doesn't need perfect leaders. It needs leaders who are honest enough to ask for the stone. And open enough to receive the hands that will hold theirs steady.

Not all strain is a sign to stop. But all strain is a signal to listen.

Churches do not always collapse under crisis. More often, they erode under the weight of silent exhaustion — leaders pushing past their limits, boards functioning on loyalty instead of alignment, congregations caught in a rhythm of "just one more thing."

But governance is not meant to be a slow surrender to fatigue. It is meant to be a practice of honest, Spirit-led sustainability.

Sometimes, the bravest move a church can make is to step back, name the truth, and invite others in.

Not with shame. Not with apology. But with clarity and faith.

God never intended any one church, pastor, board, or leader to carry the whole weight of ministry alone.

Even Moses needed help.

And so will you.

Closing Image

Picture Moses on that hill — his arms shaking, the sun still high. He doesn't speak. He doesn't command. He simply stands in his weariness. And then, Aaron appears on one side. Hur on the other.

They say nothing. They just act. A stone is placed beneath him. His arms are lifted. The people watch. And the tide of the battle shifts.

It is not the strength of one man that wins the day. It is the shared strength of a community that knows how to stand together when one cannot stand alone.

This is what Spirit-led governance looks like: Not absence of strain, but the presence of support. Not avoidance of limits, but reverence for them. Not pushing through at any cost, but moving forward — together — until the sun sets.

🌿 Discernment Questions
- Where in our ministry do we feel stretched beyond our current energy or resources?
- What are we trying to carry alone that God may be asking us to share?
- What support are we resisting — out of pride, fear, or habit?
- Who might be called to help carry part of this work?
- Are we measuring faithfulness by self-sufficiency, or by alignment with God's provision?

Chapter 6
Hearing the Silence

*Making space for sacred stillness —
where God's ongoing direction is found
in the quiet whisper*

"The Lord said, 'Go out and stand on the mountain in the presence of the Lord, for the Lord is about to pass by.' Then a great and powerful wind tore the mountains apart and shattered the rocks before the Lord, but the Lord was not in the wind.
After the wind there was an earthquake, but the Lord was not in the earthquake.
After the earthquake came a fire, but the Lord was not in the fire.
And after the fire came a gentle whisper."
– 1 Kings 19:11–12

Not every answer comes through action.
Not every season is marked by motion.
Not every leading arrives with clarity.

Sometimes, God speaks through silence.

In 1 Kings 19, the prophet Elijah stands on the edge of despair. He's given everything he has. He's endured conflict, fear, isolation. He's run for his life and landed in a cave — alone, weary, and unsure of what comes next.

God tells him to go out and stand on the mountain. To wait. To watch.

Then comes the wind. But God is not in the wind.
Then the earthquake. But God is not in the earthquake.
Then the fire. But God is not in the fire.

And then — silence.
A whisper.
A presence so subtle it can barely be named.

And that is where God is found.

This is the paradox of spiritual leadership.
We expect that clarity will come through noise — big voices, bold moves, breakthrough moments. But more often, clarity comes like it did for Elijah: **quietly, slowly, in stillness**.

Church boards are often uncomfortable with silence.
They are ready to solve. Ready to move. Ready to fix.
Meetings are full. Agendas are packed. Reports are reviewed. But the voice of God?

Often, no space is left for it.

We confuse motion with progress.
If the minutes are approved, the meeting was productive.

If no conflict arose, the board is healthy.
If action items are assigned, leadership is working.

But **discernment is not the same as decision-making.**

Discernment is not a reaction to what's urgent. It is an **attunement to what's sacred.**
It asks not, "What should we do?" but, "What is God revealing now?"

And for that question to take root, we must make space for silence. Not awkward silence. Not empty silence. But **sacred stillness** — the kind that listens before it speaks, that waits for the whisper.

Most church boards are not resistant to the Spirit.
They are simply too busy to hear it.

There is no shortage of devotion, care, or commitment in most boardrooms. What is often missing is **intentional rhythm** — a way of structuring meetings and leadership culture to make room for silence as a source of wisdom.

Silence is not what happens when no one has anything to say.
It's what happens when we **pause long enough to hear something deeper.**

This is why some boards have adopted the practice of beginning each meeting not with announcements, but with a **centering moment:**

- A breath prayer
- A slow reading of scripture
- Two minutes of silence with a candle lit
- A poem or blessing spoken aloud without response

This isn't filler. It's **preparation.**

It reminds everyone in the room that they are not just there to solve problems or pass motions. They are gathered as **spiritual stewards** — listening not only to one another, but to the quiet pull of the Spirit beneath the conversation.

Some boards go further, creating what they call **listening meetings**: gatherings with no formal agenda, held once or twice a year, meant only for:

- Prayer
- Open sharing
- Stillness
- Reflection on what God might be asking next

Others include short periods of silence between agenda items. Still others pause halfway through meetings to re-center.

There is no one right method — only the commitment to **include silence as a discipline,** not a gap.

Because silence does something extraordinary in a governance context:

- It levels power.
  In silence, no one dominates.
- It reveals hidden tension.
  In silence, what's unspoken has space to rise.
- It interrupts momentum.
  In silence, urgency loses its grip, and purpose can breathe.
- It allows the Spirit to whisper.
  Not because God wasn't speaking before — but because we finally stopped speaking long enough to hear.

None of this means the board becomes passive or indecisive. Quite the opposite.

Boards that practice silence well **make stronger decisions** — because those decisions are rooted in peace, not pressure.

When the rhythm of governance includes room for silence:

- Conflicts cool before they escalate
- Discernment becomes a habit, not a special occasion
- People feel spiritually grounded, not just operationally effective
- Creativity rises because space has been made for it to appear

Silence also reveals what needs to be let go.

Sometimes, what boards can't name with words will surface in the pause — the program that no longer has energy, the dynamic that no longer feels life-giving, the calendar that is too full for the Spirit to move freely.

Boards that listen to these silences are often the ones most able to adapt without panic.
Because they're not just reading spreadsheets or reacting to crises — they're attending to **Spirit-led truth**.

Not all silence feels holy.

Sometimes, silence feels like absence.
Sometimes, it feels like failure.

Boards that are wired for action — that pride themselves on getting things done — often struggle with silence because it confronts the fear that **maybe we don't know what to do next**.

And that fear can be loud.

It says:

- "We're stuck."
- "We're not moving fast enough."
- "We're supposed to have answers."
- "What if this is our fault?"

But what if the silence isn't a punishment — it's an invitation?

What if the lack of clarity isn't a signal to act faster — it's a call to **wait longer**?

This is one of the hardest truths in church leadership:

Sometimes, God's next step is **not yet revealed**.
And your job is not to guess — it's to **remain present**.

Spirit-led governance means learning to stay with the **not-knowing** without rushing to fill the gap.

This can be agonizing.

Especially when:

- Attendance is declining
- Giving is shrinking
- Volunteers are tired
- People want direction
- You feel the weight of expectation

But **rushing to action too soon** is often how churches make their most regrettable decisions.

- They hire the wrong staff person because "we needed someone."
- They launch a program they can't sustain.
- They commit to a building project before the vision is clear.
- They react to fear instead of listening to faith.

And in hindsight, many boards say:

"We knew it wasn't right — we just didn't know what else to do."

But what if waiting *is* doing something?

What if **the faithful act is to say, "We're not clear yet" — and to honor that truth?**

This is not passivity. It is spiritual maturity.

Because silence **isn't nothing**.
It is a posture of attention.

It is a form of leadership that says:

- "We will not move until the Spirit moves."
- "We trust that the way will be shown."
- "We believe that discernment takes time."

This doesn't mean endless stalling or avoidance.
It means **checking the impulse to fill space with noise**, and learning to recognize when the Spirit is still forming what's next.

Elijah didn't hear God in the wind, or the earthquake, or the fire.
All of those were **noisy, dramatic, urgent**.

But they were not where God was found.

God came in the whisper.

And if your board is too busy chasing noise, you might miss the whisper entirely.

So the discipline is this:

To remain in the discomfort of silence

To stay present in the not-yet

To trust that **when the whisper comes**, you will be able to hear it

And until then, you will wait with open hands, not anxious hearts

Boards that trust silence shape churches that trust silence.

Because the culture of the boardroom always becomes the culture of the congregation.

If the board is anxious, reactive, hurried — so too will be the wider body.
If the board avoids hard questions or rushes to easy answers, the congregation will learn to do the same.

But when a board practices stillness, openness, and slow listening, they model something deeply countercultural — and deeply faithful:

That leadership is not about control.

That the Spirit is not always loud.

That **uncertainty is not abandonment — it is incubation**.

This becomes especially important in seasons of transition:

- A pastor is retiring
- A major gift has been received
- A long-standing program is ending
- The community's needs are changing
- The board senses the church is called to something more — but doesn't know what

In these seasons, the temptation is to act fast.
To fill the gap. To ease discomfort. To **move before the way is clear**.

But wise boards know:

Vision is not generated — it is revealed.

And revelation requires space.

It requires:

- A calendar that isn't crammed
- Meetings with room to reflect
- A pace that honors the sacred, not just the strategic
- A theology of enough — that what is known today is sufficient for today

Churches that move too quickly often create more work than clarity.
They "vision" without discerning.
They fund without aligning.
They change without grounding.

But churches that **pause in trust** become something different:

- They become centered
- They become spacious
- They become willing to be surprised
- They become good soil

And people sense it.

They walk into a meeting and feel **peace**, not panic.
They read a board report and hear **clarity**, not spin.
They witness leadership that isn't trying to control the narrative — but trying to listen for the whisper.

This is not inaction. It is **a deeper form of action**.

It is governance that flows from presence, not performance.

It is what *Church Board Meetings Focused on God's Calling* describes as the "quiet center" — the place where leadership begins with listening, and only then moves into discernment and decision.

This posture doesn't eliminate hard choices.
It simply ensures that those choices are made from **alignment**, not urgency.

And when that becomes normal — when stillness is baked into the leadership culture — the congregation follows:

- People stop demanding answers the board doesn't have
- New leaders rise up without pressure
- Change becomes something organic, not reactive
- And the whisper of God becomes something everyone is listening for

Not because they were told to.
But because the leaders showed them how.

Silence is not the absence of leadership — it is the presence of listening.

Churches need leaders who can speak clearly — but also leaders who can wait quietly.
Not out of fear. Not out of avoidance.
But out of a deep trust that **Spirit-led timing matters**.

Sometimes, the most faithful thing a board can do is to **create space**.
Not because there's nothing to say — but because something deeper needs to be heard.

When silence is welcomed — not as an interruption, but as an ally —

the board becomes a place where wisdom can rise without being forced.

Closing Image

Picture a boardroom with nothing on the table but a candle and a single question:

"What is the Spirit saying now?"

No one speaks right away.
The papers are set aside. The spreadsheet is still open, but no one is looking at it.
The room is quiet — not because no one has ideas, but because everyone is listening.
There's a sense of weight — not heavy, but sacred.

And then someone exhales.
And someone else prays.
And a next step begins to form — not from a quick answer, but from the **quiet ground of trust.**

This is not just spiritual reflection.
It is governance at its most faithful.

🕊 Discernment Questions

- Where in our leadership rhythm is there room for silence?
- Do we treat stillness as valuable — or as wasted time?
- Are we creating space for the Spirit to speak — or only space for ourselves to speak?
- What decisions or conversations need more time in stillness before we move forward?
- How can we model trust in the whisper — especially when others want clarity now?

Part Two: Structures That Support the Call

"Write the vision; make it plain on tablets, so that a runner may read it."

– Habakkuk 2:2

Part Two: Structures That Support the Call

This section focuses on the systems and structures that sustain a healthy church. Governance, bylaws, board roles, and decision-making processes all exist to support—not stifle—the movement of the Spirit in our congregations.

- Forming Our Structure
- The Rule of Love
- Keeping the Wolves at Bay
- Faithful Over a Little
- Building Trust Through Transparency

Chapter 7
Wisdom That Builds the House

Establishing governance culture and practices that reflect spiritual maturity and faith

"By wisdom a house is built and by understanding it is established; by knowledge the rooms are filled with all precious and peasant riches."
— Proverbs 24:3–4

Some churches try to build structure first. They start with bylaws, draft elaborate policies, set meeting schedules, and name officers. And yet, despite all that structure, the house doesn't feel steady. Meetings are tense or aimless. Decisions get bogged down. People show up out of duty, not joy. The structure exists, but the spirit of the structure is missing. Others avoid structure altogether. They say, "We're led by the Spirit," or "We don't want to be too formal," or "We've always done it this way." And for a time, that can work. But as the church grows or changes, what once felt like freedom becomes confusion. Roles blur. Authority gets concentrated in the loudest voices. And those with wisdom often step back, unsure where they fit in. Scripture reminds us that wisdom builds the house. Not just rules. Not just freedom. Wisdom. And the wisdom of governance—spiritually grounded, lovingly practiced, and clearly articulated—is what allows a church to grow in both faith and function. The goal of good structure is not control. It is capacity. Capacity to respond to God's call. Capacity to support leaders well. Capacity to grow without losing integrity. A wise house is not rigid. It is spacious and strong. It holds the sacred tension between order and openness. Between roles and relationships. Between discernment and action. In this chapter, we'll explore how churches can form governance structures that reflect spiritual maturity—not just institutional efficiency. Structures that are not merely inherited, but intentional. Structures that create room for the Spirit to fill the house.

Every church has a governance culture—even if it's never been named. Some congregations operate like informal families, with decisions made relationally and leadership concentrated in a few long-standing members. Others lean heavily on procedure, with tightly defined rules and formal hierarchies. Most fall somewhere in between. But whether a church is conscious of it or not, the governance culture it lives into shapes everything from how decisions are made to how people feel about serving. Governance culture is not just about documents. It is about the way authority is practiced. It includes how meetings are led, how leadership is shared, how disagreement is handled, and how faithfully the church stays aligned to its Calling. A spiritually mature governance culture is marked by clarity, humility, and discernment. It doesn't need to dominate or retreat. It listens. It adapts. It honors roles while remaining open to Spirit-led change. Building that kind of culture begins with reflection. Who makes decisions in your church—and how? Are roles clear or assumed? Is there trust that the process reflects the Spirit's movement, or frustration that things seem stuck or siloed? Are meetings spiritual moments or mere formalities? These questions help unearth what has been inherited, and what may need to be reshaped. Structure should be a reflection of Calling—not the other way around. Churches that focus too heavily on structure before seeking spiritual clarity may end up managing systems that no longer serve their mission. But churches that discern their Calling and then build structure to support it can create a faithful, functional foundation.

Establishing a healthy governance structure is not about copying a template from another congregation. It's about designing a framework that aligns with the specific Calling, gifts, and needs of your church. This begins with a clear understanding of what governance is and what it is not. Governance is the practice of shared spiritual leadership. It is the way a community discerns direction, stewards resources, protects its integrity, and holds one another accountable to its shared commitments. It is not about power. It is about trust. A wise structure reflects this. It outlines roles without hierarchy. It defines responsibilities without micromanagement. It allows decisions to be made in a timely, transparent, and collaborative way. And it grounds all of this in prayerful discernment and communal wisdom. One of the first steps in forming such a structure is to revisit the congregation's foundational documents—bylaws, policies, role descriptions—and ask whether they reflect the current Calling and energy of the church. Bylaws that once made sense in a larger or smaller congregation may now hinder healthy function. Policies that were drafted in a different era may no longer support the current realities of ministry. And roles that are poorly defined or outdated often leave volunteers overwhelmed or unsure how to serve. Rather than treating these documents as untouchable, churches should see them as living tools—subject to periodic review and revision as the Spirit leads. This is not a matter of disrespecting tradition, but of honoring it by allowing it to breathe.

Churches that embrace governance as spiritual practice often adopt habits that keep structure aligned with mission. One of the most important is regular board self-assessment. A spiritually mature board asks not only "Are we following the rules?" but also "Are our structures serving our Calling?" This may involve an annual review of bylaws and policies, but it also includes deeper questions: Are our meetings designed for discernment or just updates? Do we distribute leadership well, or are decisions concentrated in just a few people? Are our processes accessible to newer members, or do they rely on unwritten norms? Assessment helps identify both the strengths and the strains in the system—before crisis forces change. Another wise practice is role clarity. Many churches assume everyone knows who does what, until something falls through the cracks. Clear role descriptions—whether for officers, committee chairs, or staff—help distribute work fairly and empower people to serve with confidence. But these descriptions must also evolve. As churches shift from program-based to mission-based ministry, leadership needs shift too. Reviewing roles annually and allowing room for adjustment is part of healthy governance. Meetings themselves should also reflect spiritual maturity. This doesn't mean they must be long or overly formal. But it does mean they are prepared for thoughtfully, led with intention, and grounded in the spiritual life of the community.

Good meetings are not just about decisions—they are moments of discernment, trust-building, and shared responsibility.

Another hallmark of spiritually mature governance is how the board approaches conflict. In churches with weak or overly rigid structures, conflict either festers or explodes. But in churches with wise governance, conflict becomes an opportunity for growth. A well-formed structure provides the tools to navigate tension without personalizing it. It includes clear expectations, processes for decision-making, and agreed-upon norms for communication. These structures don't prevent conflict, but they prevent confusion—and confusion is often what turns disagreement into division. When leaders trust the process, they can focus on listening to each other and to the Spirit, rather than defending turf or reacting from fear. Spiritually mature governance also pays attention to succession. Wisdom builds not only for today but for tomorrow. A wise house prepares future leaders. This means intentionally mentoring new members, inviting younger or less experienced individuals into leadership spaces, and designing systems that allow for healthy transition. Churches that fail to do this often find themselves caught off guard when longtime leaders step down. But when governance includes succession planning as a spiritual responsibility, it creates continuity without control. Governance practices become a form of discipleship, and leadership becomes a shared, sustainable ministry. Ultimately, governance that reflects spiritual maturity is not flashy. It is faithful. It is marked by consistency, integrity, and quiet strength. And like a well-built house, it holds the weight of ministry not with strain, but with grace.

Churches often fall into predictable traps when trying to improve their governance. One common error is over-correcting. A church that has operated too informally might suddenly adopt rigid rules and procedures in an effort to "fix" what feels broken. Another congregation, burned by conflict, may swing the other way—removing formal structure in hopes of fostering peace. But either extreme leads to imbalance. Wisdom calls for nuance. Healthy structure is not reactive—it is reflective. It grows from a clear sense of the church's Calling, and it is built to serve that Calling with both flexibility and strength. Another trap is equating structure with bureaucracy. Spiritual governance does not require layers of committees or complicated procedures. In fact, the most effective structures are often simple. What matters is not how many policies a church has, but whether those policies reflect discernment, encourage participation, and foster accountability. A board that meets monthly with prayer, clarity of purpose, and shared responsibility is often more faithful—and more effective—than one that follows Roberts Rules perfectly but lacks spiritual grounding. Forming a wise governance structure also means paying attention to how meetings are experienced. Are board members prepared in advance, or reading materials on the spot? Are decisions made collaboratively, or deferred to the most vocal? Do members feel their gifts are being used, or that they are filling a seat out of obligation? These questions help assess not only the function but the feel of governance. A spiritually mature structure will always elevate dignity and shared purpose.

Spiritual posture matters as much as process. A church may have excellent bylaws and clear role descriptions, but if the posture of the board is anxious, controlling, or distracted, the structure will serve fear instead of faith. Governance, at its best, is a ministry of presence. Leaders come not only with their skills, but with their spiritual attention. They show up grounded in prayer, open to the Spirit, and committed to one another's growth. This kind of posture transforms the tone of meetings. It shifts the focus from "getting through the agenda" to asking, "How is God calling us to lead faithfully right now?" One church, for example, began opening every board meeting with ten minutes of silence followed by a reading from their discerned Calling statement. At first, it felt awkward. But over time, it changed the culture. Leaders spoke with more humility. Decisions were less reactive. People began to name tensions before they escalated. The structure hadn't changed—but the spirit within it had. Another congregation made a practice of reviewing their leadership covenant before major decisions. The covenant included commitments like listening deeply, assuming good intent, and pausing when emotions ran high. This helped them navigate difficult conversations about staffing and finances without fracturing trust. These churches didn't just update their policies. They cultivated governance cultures rooted in spiritual maturity. That's the real work of forming a wise house. It's not about building walls—it's about shaping a container where the Spirit can dwell and guide.

Wise governance is not built in a day. It is formed slowly, through seasons of discernment, trial, adaptation, and trust. It is shaped as leaders grow in spiritual maturity—not only in their knowledge of procedure, but in their willingness to serve one another with humility and care. Over time, structure becomes less about rules and more about rhythm. Meetings become less about reports and more about renewal. Governance becomes less about authority and more about accountability to God's vision for the church. This transformation doesn't happen by accident. It requires intentional cultivation. It means choosing to value preparation over spontaneity, discernment over expedience, and faithfulness over efficiency. It means training new leaders not only in roles but in posture. It means pausing to review what has been inherited, and having the courage to reshape what no longer reflects your shared Calling. And it means holding structure lightly—firm enough to support ministry, flexible enough to follow Spirit. When a church commits to this path, the results are visible. Meetings feel purposeful. Disagreements are navigated with grace. Leaders stay longer, and give more freely of themselves. New members find it easier to join and serve. And the whole congregation benefits from the steady pulse of wise leadership. Proverbs reminds us: wisdom builds the house. It is not rushed. It is not loud. It is not easily swayed by urgency or trend. But it creates a place of strength and beauty—where Calling is honored, energy is well stewarded, and resources are used in faithful service of God's work in the world.

Closing Image

Picture a home—not brand new, but well-lived-in. The walls hold stories. The beams bear the weight of love and challenge. It creaks a little, but it stands strong. Not because it was built quickly or perfectly, but because it was built wisely. With care. With intention. With faith that what is formed with understanding will last. Governance, like that home, doesn't have to impress. It only needs to endure. And when wisdom builds the house, the Spirit finds room to dwell within.

🕊 Discernment Questions

- What unspoken values shape our current governance culture?
- Where might our structures be serving old habits rather than our current Calling?
- Do our board meetings reflect spiritual maturity or merely procedural compliance?
- How are we preparing the next generation of leaders to carry forward wise governance?
- What small changes could better align our structure with the Spirit's guidance?

Chapter 8
Forming Our Structure

Developing bylaws, roles, and systems that support and protect faithful leadership

"I left you behind in Crete for this reason, so that you should put in order what remained to be done..."
– Titus 1:5

"You should also look for able men among all the people, men who fear God, are trustworthy, and hate dishonest gain... Let them sit as judges for the people at all times; make it easier for yourself, and they will bear the burden with you."
– Exodus 18:21–23

Structure is not the enemy of the Spirit. When rightly formed, structure is a vessel—a framework that helps us sustain the Calling entrusted to us.

From the earliest days of the church, structure was necessary. Paul instructs Titus to "put in order what remained to be done." Moses is counseled by his father-in-law to share the burden of leadership, not to carry it alone. In both cases, God's Calling required something more than inspiration. It required systems that could support sustained faithfulness.

Many congregations treat bylaws, role descriptions, and policies as dry technical documents, only to be consulted in conflict. But what if these governing tools were understood not as constraints, but as **instruments of care**?

What if structure was an act of stewardship?

To fulfill God's Calling, the energy of leadership must be protected. That protection comes not through control, but through clarity—clear roles, clear authority, clear accountability. When these are absent, leadership becomes reactive. Resources are wasted. The Spirit's movement is often missed because leaders are buried in confusion.

This chapter explores how to form a structure that **protects leadership**, **aligns energy**, and **focuses resources** on the work God has entrusted to the church. We begin with the foundation: bylaws.

- Why bylaws must evolve alongside the congregation's current Calling
- How to distinguish between helpful guardrails and restrictive rigidity
- The role of board chairs, nominating committees, and pastoral relations in healthy structural alignment

Bylaws Are Not the Gospel—But They Protect It

Your church's bylaws are not scripture. But they are sacred in the sense that they hold space for what God is doing in your midst.

When crafted well, bylaws help congregations clarify decision-making authority, define leadership roles, and create consistent processes that free up energy for mission. They don't replace prayerful discernment—they support it. They help ensure that leadership transitions are healthy, that responsibilities are distributed wisely, and that your energy is not spent constantly reinventing systems that should already be in place.

But bylaws must evolve. Too many churches are bound by language written in a different era, for a different congregation. When bylaws are misaligned with current needs, people begin to work around them—or ignore them altogether. Over time, this leads to confusion, conflict, and sometimes even legal vulnerability.

Updating your bylaws is not an act of rebellion. It is an act of responsibility.

If God is calling your church into new forms of ministry, new expressions of leadership, or new partnerships in your community—your structure must adapt to support that call. Holding on to outdated documents "because that's how it's always been" is not faithfulness. It's fear.

The governing body bears the responsibility of ensuring that the church's structure continues to reflect its current Calling—not just its history.

Roles That Safeguard the Calling

At the heart of good governance is the question: *How will we structure ourselves to hear and respond to God's Call?*

This is not about micromanagement or hierarchy. It is about discernment. And discernment requires clarity—especially in leadership roles.

A well-formed structure defines roles not just to assign tasks, but to **protect the purpose** of those who serve. It ensures the governing body chair is empowered to lead without being isolated, that the nominating process reflects the diversity and gifts of the congregation, and that pastors are supported—not evaluated—by relational structures rooted in trust.

Each of these functions serves a spiritual purpose.

The Board Chair: Keeper of Clarity

The board chair is not the boss. The chair is the *keeper of clarity*. Their role is to guide meetings with integrity, keep the focus on mission, and create space for diverse voices while helping the group move forward in unity.

A chair leads best when:

- The agenda is aligned with Calling
- Time is protected for prayerful discussion
- Decisions are documented clearly
- Disagreements are honored without becoming divisions

The chair also protects the spiritual rhythm of governance by pacing decisions, preventing burnout, and ensuring that business does not replace discernment. When this role is held with intention, it strengthens the energy of the entire board.

The Nominating Process: A Sacred Invitation

Too often, nominating committees are seen as functional task forces. But they are spiritual discernment teams. They are entrusted with identifying those whom God is calling into leadership—and inviting them to respond.

This work is not just about filling vacancies. It is about listening for gifts. It is about seeing potential. It is about ensuring that the board reflects the **fullness of the Body of Christ**—across age, race, ability, and background.

Good nominating work asks:

- What gifts are needed on the board in this season of our Calling?
- Who among us is being shaped to offer those gifts?
- Are we inviting people into leadership with clarity, honesty, and care?

Structure matters here. When the process is rushed, vague, or overly politicized, the entire congregation suffers. But when it is grounded in prayer and purpose, it can bring forth new life.

The Pastoral Relations Committee: A Listening Structure

A strong structure does not just define who decides—it also defines who listens.

The Pastoral Relations Committee (PRC) is one of the most overlooked but essential structures for protecting both leadership and the congregation. It is not a performance review team. It is not a complaint box. It is a **relational bridge**, a place where the pastor and congregation can build trust, tend wounds, and explore how the Spirit is shaping their shared life.

A healthy PRC meets regularly. It holds confidences. It listens without defensiveness. It honors the complexity of pastoral leadership and helps the pastor reflect, rest, and re-engage with clarity.

When churches lack this structure, pastors often feel alone, and the congregation may have no safe place to process concerns before they become crises. But with a PRC in place, the congregation's energy is aligned with care—and care becomes part of the structure.

Policies and Procedures: Writing the Vision Plain

Structure is not only about who does what. It's also about how things are done—consistently, faithfully, and in alignment with the church's values. Policies and procedures provide that consistency. They are not legalistic constraints, but written expressions of trust. When leaders know what is expected, and when responsibilities are clearly defined, energy is no longer wasted on confusion. Time and focus are preserved for ministry.

This is why Exodus 18 matters. Moses is advised to delegate leadership so that he does not grow weary—and so the people are served more faithfully. But that delegation required clarity. Those who were entrusted with responsibility had to know what they were being asked to do. Written policies make that clarity possible. They make expectations visible, transferable, and sustainable.

Good policies do not micromanage. They describe what the church values, why it matters, and how it should be carried out. Good procedures do not overwhelm—they guide. They create patterns of faithful behavior that can be followed by new leaders as easily as seasoned ones.

This is especially important when it comes to financial policies, pastoral care structures, child safety protocols, and governance processes. When policies are in place, they reduce conflict, increase trust, and create a culture where decisions are made not by guesswork or memory, but by shared understanding.

Churches that neglect written procedures often find themselves reinventing the wheel—or worse, relying on unspoken norms that change with each leader. But churches that invest in thoughtful policy development protect their Calling. They ensure that energy flows toward ministry—not confusion. And they use their resources in alignment with God's purpose.

Closing Image:
Picture a foundation being poured. Not flashy. Not visible when the building rises. But essential. Without it, the structure will crack. With it, everything holds. Your bylaws are not about control — they're about capacity. They create space for mission to be sustained, even when the faces around the table change.

🌱 Discernment Questions:

- Do our current bylaws reflect who we are now and what we're called to do?
- Where have we avoided necessary updates out of fear or complexity?
- What bylaws create flexibility for mission—and which ones hold us back?
- How do our governance documents support healthy leadership transitions?

Chapter 9
Sealed In Covenant

Using behavioral covenants and board agreements to clarify expectations and foster trust

"Because of all this we make a firm agreement in writing, and on that sealed document are inscribed the names of our officials, our Levites, and our priests."

– Nehemiah 9:38

Some church boards struggle not because they lack faith, vision, or commitment—but because they never named what they expected from each other. Assumptions creep in. Trust erodes. Conflicts linger just beneath the surface. Without shared agreements, even the most prayerful board can become uncertain about how to lead together. Behavioral covenants and board agreements are not legal documents. They are spiritual tools. They name how a group chooses to live, serve, and discern together. They clarify expectations not just about tasks, but about trust, communication, participation, and respect. And when things get hard—and they always do—it is these shared agreements that help the board stay grounded. In the book of Nehemiah, after a long season of rebuilding and repentance, the leaders of the people make a covenant. It is not just a private promise—it is a written agreement, sealed with names. It reflects their shared accountability and sacred intention. In the same way, behavioral covenants in church governance are a way of sealing the board's commitment to lead with integrity, compassion, and care. These covenants do not replace bylaws. They enliven them. Where bylaws define structure, behavioral covenants define culture. Where policies manage decisions, covenants guide behavior. Both are needed. But only one speaks to the spirit with which we lead.

A covenant begins with conversation. Not just about what the board does, but how it does it. How do we speak to each other when we disagree? What do we expect when someone cannot attend a meeting? How do we handle conflict, fatigue, or frustration? What kind of tone do we want to set—for each other and for the congregation we serve? These questions surface the unspoken norms that already exist, and invite the board to name which ones to carry forward and which to release. Some boards avoid creating covenants because it feels too formal or unnecessary. But clarity is not control—it is kindness. When expectations are clear, people can serve with freedom. When they are vague, people feel anxious or misaligned. Covenant language does not need to be complex. In fact, the most effective covenants are simple. One church began each year by reaffirming five shared commitments: Speak truth in love. Assume good intent. Show up prepared. Listen with humility. Take responsibility for what is ours. These five phrases shaped the entire board culture. When someone interrupted or checked out or responded harshly, the chair could gently ask, "Does this align with our covenant?" It wasn't about blame. It was about remembering who they wanted to be. Another board wrote their covenant around the fruits of the Spirit. Each member reflected on what it meant to bring love, joy, peace, patience, kindness, goodness, faithfulness, gentleness, and self-control to their leadership. When conflict arose, they asked: Which fruit is missing right now? This simple practice kept their conversations rooted in scripture and grounded in grace.

Behavioral covenants are especially powerful during seasons of transition, conflict, or growth. In times of change, anxiety often rises. People make assumptions. Communication gets reactive. Covenant provides an anchor. It gives the board something to return to—a shared understanding of how they will treat one another, even when emotions run high or opinions diverge. But covenants are not just reactive tools. They are also proactive. They build trust before it is tested. They help new members acclimate quickly. They prevent drift by keeping spiritual maturity at the center of governance. And they remind the board that how we lead is just as important as what we decide. A common question is whether covenants should be written down. The answer is yes. Not because written words are magic, but because memory fades. A written covenant creates shared accountability. It allows members to revisit and reflect. It invites intentional recommitment. Some churches include their covenant at the beginning of every meeting packet. Others read it aloud quarterly. Some review and update it annually as part of board orientation. The goal is not to create a rigid script, but a living reminder. Covenants are not meant to constrain. They are meant to clarify. They protect the spiritual tone of leadership. They keep power rooted in prayer. They guard the board from the silent erosion of trust that so often undermines ministry. And they invite each leader to bring their best self—not just their vote or voice, but their character, to the table.

Board agreements are a close companion to behavioral covenants, but with a slightly different focus. Where covenants speak to culture and character, board agreements clarify expectations around logistics, roles, and responsibilities. These agreements might address things like attendance, preparation, confidentiality, communication between meetings, or processes for decision-making. They help answer questions like: How often will we meet? What do we expect of each other between meetings? How will we communicate urgency or disagreement? What happens if someone is consistently unengaged? These agreements are especially important for churches with rotating leadership or term limits. They provide continuity amid change. They ensure that every board member, new or seasoned, knows what it means to serve well. And they create shared standards for accountability. One church adopted a practice of reviewing and re-signing its board agreement at the first meeting of every new year. It included expectations about attendance, confidentiality, mutual respect, preparation, and willingness to speak the truth in love. When a conflict emerged midyear, the board was able to return to that agreement, not as a weapon, but as a mirror. It allowed them to ask: Are we honoring what we said we would do? Are we still leading the way we promised? These moments of return are sacred. They turn governance into a spiritual practice—not just a technical one. They remind the board that accountability is not about shame. It is about shared commitment, revisited in love.

For behavioral covenants and board agreements to be effective, they must be created collaboratively. Documents handed down from previous boards or drafted by one person rarely carry the same weight as those formed through shared discernment. The process of creating the covenant is just as important as the content. It invites honest conversation. It surfaces past wounds and future hopes. It gives the board a chance to name who they have been and who they are called to become. Facilitating these conversations requires spiritual sensitivity. It may begin with prayer and scripture. It may include small group discussion or silent reflection. It should allow space for disagreement, revision, and storytelling. What matters most is that every board member feels heard, and that the final document reflects shared values—not just best practices, but lived commitments. Once adopted, the covenant and board agreement should not be forgotten. They should be integrated into the rhythm of governance. New board members should be oriented to them. Conflicts should be interpreted through them. Meetings should be shaped by them. And boards should make space regularly to reflect on them. Are we living our covenant? Are we honoring our agreement? Where do we need to recommit? Where do we need to forgive? These are not just operational questions. They are spiritual questions. Because the board is not simply an organizational body. It is a community of leaders, called together, entrusted with the care of a congregation. And like any spiritual community, it requires covenant to thrive.

In Nehemiah's time, the people of God faced a defining moment. After exile and return, after ruin and rebuilding, they chose to seal their renewed commitment in writing. Not because the words alone would protect them, but because the act of naming and agreeing mattered. It made their devotion visible. It called them to account. And it bound them to one another with sacred intention. So it is with boards today. When a governing body commits itself to a behavioral covenant and board agreement, it does more than set expectations. It declares that how we lead matters. That trust is worth tending. That clarity is an act of care. That spiritual maturity includes accountability. A covenant does not prevent every misunderstanding. An agreement does not guarantee perfect behavior. But together, they give the board tools to navigate hard seasons with grace. They offer a shared language for correction and growth. They help boards stay grounded—not just in policy, but in purpose. When these tools are practiced over time, they shape a leadership culture of transparency, resilience, and love. Leaders are less likely to burn out. Conflicts are less likely to escalate. Meetings feel safer, decisions come easier, and the work of governance becomes a witness to the Spirit's presence in the life of the church. Sealing our leadership in covenant is not a formality. It is a form of faithfulness. It is how we say to each other: I will show up. I will speak the truth. I will listen with grace. I will walk beside you, even when it's hard. And together, we will lead as those who belong to God.

Closing Image

Imagine a circle of leaders standing together—not in uniform, not in rank, but in mutual trust. In their hands is a shared document, not legal in tone but sacred in intent. One by one, they add their names. Not as signatures of status, but as symbols of belonging. This is not just a covenant—it is a declaration: We choose to lead with integrity. We choose to listen with grace. We choose to hold one another, and be held. Not perfectly—but faithfully. Together.

Discernment Questions

- What expectations about board behavior have remained unspoken in our leadership culture?
- How might a covenant help us clarify how we want to lead together?
- When conflict or confusion arises, do we have a shared agreement to guide our response?
- Are our current board norms forming a culture of trust—or tolerating patterns that erode it?
- How might we create or renew a covenant that reflects who we are and who we are called to become?

Chapter 10
Meeting in the Presence of God

Transforming board meetings into sacred spaces for discernment, planning, and prayer

"For where two or three are gathered in my name, I am there among them."
– Matthew 18:20

Church board meetings are often imagined as places of business. Agendas are distributed. Reports are reviewed. Motions are made. And somewhere along the way, the original purpose gets lost. What should be a moment of collective discernment becomes a rush to finish the agenda. What should feel like worship feels like weariness. Yet Jesus promised: "Where two or three are gathered in my name, I am there among them." That includes the boardroom. That includes the budget meeting. That includes the long Tuesday night with coffee cups and paper stacks and prayer requests. This chapter invites us to reclaim that sacred space—not by abandoning structure, but by infusing structure with Spirit. The work of governance is holy. It shapes the direction of the church. It stewards the energy and resources of God's people. And when done with prayer, presence, and discernment, it becomes an extension of worship. Not every decision is spiritual. But every meeting can be.

To treat board meetings as sacred, we must first shift our posture. We are not gathering simply to manage the church. We are gathering to listen—to God, to one another, and to the Spirit's leading among us. That listening begins before the meeting starts. Spirit-led meetings are not just about the agenda. They begin with spiritual preparation. The chair or facilitator is not merely a timekeeper—they are a spiritual leader, stewarding the tone and focus of the gathering. Opening each meeting with intentional prayer, silence, or scripture creates space for presence. One church began each meeting by reading their mission statement aloud. Another lit a candle and paused for a moment of stillness. Another invited members to name something they were grateful for before moving into discussion. These small rituals re-center the board. They remind leaders that this is not just another task on a long list. It is a moment of sacred responsibility. Preparation also includes setting an agenda that reflects the church's Calling. According to best practices shared in *Church Board Meetings Focused on God's*

Calling, every agenda should highlight which items are for discernment, which are for decision, and which are for information. Items related to the church's mission should take priority. Time should be assigned to each section to encourage focus, not haste. The agenda becomes more than a list—it becomes a tool of intention.

Effective facilitation plays a vital role in honoring the Spirit's presence. The facilitator—or board chair—is not just responsible for keeping the meeting moving. They are responsible for helping the board stay spiritually grounded, mission-focused, and relationally healthy. That begins by naming expectations at the start. What tone do we want to set? What rules of engagement are we holding? Are we prepared to listen with grace, speak with clarity, and stay open to the Spirit's movement, even if it disrupts our plans? These are not procedural questions. They are spiritual postures. The best facilitators are impartial and prayerful. They ensure everyone is heard, not just the loudest voices. They watch the room for signs of fatigue, distraction, or tension. They return the group to mission when the discussion drifts. And they model humility when strong opinions arise. Facilitation also means paying attention to pace. Meetings that drag wear down energy and spiritual attentiveness. Meetings that rush miss opportunities for discernment. Setting time expectations for each item and using a designated timekeeper can help balance flow and depth. Good facilitation doesn't remove the Spirit—it makes room for it. When meetings are well-structured and gently led, the board can focus more fully on the matters of God's Calling. There is less confusion. Less repetition. Less anxiety. And more clarity about what is needed now.

Discernment is the heartbeat of spiritually grounded meetings. It is not the same as consensus. It is not simply compromise. Discernment is the practice of collectively seeking God's wisdom.

It requires preparation, humility, and time. Some decisions are clear. Others are complex. A board grounded in spiritual maturity will not rush when the Spirit says wait, and will not hesitate when the Spirit says move. That requires trust—not only in each other, but in the process. One tool many boards have found helpful is the practice of pausing. When a difficult topic arises, or when disagreement is sharp, the facilitator might call for a moment of silence. This gives space for emotion to settle and for Spirit to speak. Some boards designate space on the agenda for open-ended discernment questions: What is God asking of us in this moment? What does our Calling require of us? What is the risk of inaction? What is the deeper issue beneath this conversation? These questions redirect focus from logistics to meaning. They make space for wisdom to emerge—not just from the experts, but from the collective body. And when decisions are made, boards can move forward with deeper unity and confidence, having listened together for the Spirit's direction.

Prayer must be woven throughout the meeting—not confined to the beginning or end. It is the breath of the board's work. Prayer grounds conversations in grace. It interrupts anxiety. It reminds the board that they are not alone in leading. When prayer is integrated throughout the meeting, it transforms the energy of the room. A board member may be invited to offer a prayer before a major decision. Someone might pause to pray over a challenging situation or conflict. At the close of a difficult conversation, the chair might ask for silent prayer or a collective blessing. These practices do not have to be elaborate. What matters is intention. The Spirit does not require polished words—only honest hearts. Boards that pray together build trust together. They learn to hold space for one another. They grow in their capacity to listen—not just to each other, but to God. Over time, meetings shift. They become more than functional. They become formational. The board is not just making decisions. It is being shaped—into a body that listens, responds, and leads with faithfulness.

Integrating sacred rhythms into board meetings also means creating space for reflection and renewal. Not every meeting should be packed with decisions. Some gatherings should be designed for retreat, review, or realignment. This may look like setting aside time each quarter to reflect on what has been learned, where the Spirit has shown up, and what shifts may be needed. It may involve reviewing the church's Calling statement and asking: Are we still aligned? Has our energy shifted? Are we stewarding our resources faithfully? These rhythms keep governance from becoming mechanical. They allow the board to return to its spiritual center. They remind leaders that governance is not just about managing the present—it is about listening for the future. Boards that adopt a rhythm of reflection often experience deeper unity and longer-term impact. They make better decisions not because they have better tools, but because they have clearer hearts. And when the church sees that its leaders are guided by prayer, shaped by discernment, and grounded in mission, it fosters trust across the whole body.

When we treat meetings as sacred space, we are not romanticizing the work—we are re-sanctifying it. We are remembering that leadership in the church is not just organizational. It is spiritual. Every meeting is a chance to embody the love, humility, and attentiveness of Christ. Every agenda is a chance to realign with God's mission. Every discussion is a chance to grow in grace. Jesus promised to be present when two or three gather in His name. That promise is not reserved for worship services alone. It is alive in the boardroom, the budget meeting, the conflict conversation, and the long, slow discernment of next steps. When church leaders gather with intention, with prayer, and with openness to the Spirit, they do more than govern. They become vessels of God's guidance. The room becomes a sanctuary. The conversation becomes liturgy. And the board becomes a community of stewards, faithfully tending to the unfolding work of God's Calling in their midst.

Closing Image

Picture a candle on a table. Its flame flickers gently as papers rustle and voices rise and fall. Around that table sit people entrusted with sacred responsibility. Their titles vary. Their perspectives differ. But together, they lean toward something greater. The agenda is before them. The Spirit is among them. And as they speak, pause, pray, and decide—they do so not as managers, but as stewards. Not just of tasks, but of trust. Not just of time, but of the holy unfolding of God's work in their midst.

🕊 Discernment Questions

- Do our meetings reflect the presence of Christ—or simply the pressure of leadership?
- How might we prepare ourselves spiritually before gathering to make decisions?
- What practices could help us listen more deeply for the Spirit during our meetings?
- Are our agendas shaped by Calling, or driven by habit and urgency?
- In what ways might prayer, silence, or reflection strengthen our board's spiritual posture?

Chapter 11
Movement Leads to Stillness

Developing rhythms of reflection, responsiveness, and spiritual attentiveness in governance

"I will stand at my watchpost, and station myself on the rampart; I will keep watch to see what he will say to me."
– Habakkuk 2:1

"The Lord came and stood there, calling as before, "Samuel! Samuel!" And Samuel said, "Speak, for your servant is listening."
– 1 Samuel 3:10

"Be still, and know that I am God."
– Psalm 46:10

Now beginning the chapter itself, fully aligned with the tone, formatting, and delivery style of *Embracing Our Call*. No line breaks will be used.

Leadership often feels like motion. There are agendas to finalize, reports to review, decisions to make, and people to engage. Church boards are full of movement—calendar movement, financial movement, ministry movement. But faithful governance is not measured by how much we do. It is measured by whether we pause long enough to hear what God is asking us to do. In scripture, movement and stillness are not opposites. They are rhythms. God speaks in the burning bush and in the whisper. God moves through the storm and in the silence that follows. Spirit-led governance is not about speed—it is about attentiveness. This chapter explores the rhythms of reflection and responsiveness that allow boards to lead from a posture of spiritual maturity. It asks: When do we pause? How do we listen? What space have we created for the Spirit to speak? And how do we let that voice shape what comes next?

The prophet Habakkuk offers a striking image: "I will stand at my watchpost... I will keep watch to see what he will say to me." Governance rooted in discernment begins here—with the willingness to watch and wait. In many churches, governance has become reactive. Meetings are driven by urgent updates or long-standing to-do lists. Decisions are made quickly, sometimes defensively, and the space for prayerful reflection is lost. But God's guidance is rarely found in haste. It requires posture, patience, and pause. Boards that lead with spiritual attentiveness build in rhythms of stillness. This does not mean every meeting is slow or passive. It means that within the rhythm of leadership, there is intentional time set aside to listen—not just to one another, but to God. This might take the form of reflective silence before major decisions. It might be a practice of reading scripture aloud before reviewing the agenda. Some boards reserve the first fifteen minutes of each meeting for spiritual check-in: Where have we seen God at work in the life of the church this month? Where have we felt tension or unease? What do we sense the Spirit nudging us to pay attention to? These practices may seem small, but over time, they cultivate a different kind of leadership. One that moves not from pressure, but from Presence.

Boards that embrace rhythms of reflection do not lose effectiveness—they gain clarity. When leaders pause to reflect, they are better able to recognize patterns, identify where energy is being drained, and celebrate where God's grace is sustaining the work. Reflection is not indulgent. It is essential. A church that never reflects risks drifting. A board that never listens risks leading from assumption rather than alignment. Rhythmic reflection creates spiritual muscle memory. It helps the board remain responsive rather than reactive. Responsiveness is different from efficiency. Efficiency asks, "What's the quickest path forward?" Responsiveness asks, "What is God asking of us now?" The difference is subtle but profound. Responsive boards pay attention to timing—not just deadlines, but divine nudges. They may choose to pause on a decision that feels unclear. They may notice a recurring theme across multiple reports and decide to explore it further. They may shift priorities mid-year because discernment has revealed a deeper need. This kind of flexibility is only possible when a board is grounded in stillness. Stillness creates space for responsiveness. It slows the rush to act and creates room to perceive. It reminds the board that their task is not only to lead, but to follow—to follow the movement of the Spirit, which often flows beneath the surface of plans and reports.

The story of young Samuel offers a powerful model. God speaks, but Samuel does not yet know how to listen. It is only when Eli helps him recognize the voice that Samuel responds, "Speak, for your servant is listening." Church boards, too, must cultivate the ability to recognize the Spirit's voice amid the noise of leadership.

That recognition comes with practice. It comes with quiet. It comes with the humility to admit we don't always know what's best. Governance meetings can easily fill with tasks—budgets, building maintenance, staff reviews, upcoming events. These are important. But without space for stillness, the board risks losing its spiritual center. What would it look like for your board to say, in the middle of a meeting, "Speak, Lord, for your servants are listening"? What decisions might shift? What assumptions might soften? What direction might change? Stillness is not inactivity. It is intentional receptivity. It is the act of laying down control long enough to hear something deeper than opinion or strategy. Psalm 46:10 does not suggest we stop working forever. It invites us to **be still and know.** Know what is true. Know who is God. Know what is ours to do. And just as importantly, know what is not.

Boards that practice spiritual attentiveness create a different kind of culture—one marked by humility, clarity, and peace. These boards are not easily shaken by conflict or urgency because they have learned how to pause. They are not driven by ego because they are grounded in prayer. They do not make decisions to avoid discomfort but to remain faithful. Reflection is woven into their rhythm. They schedule retreats not as an afterthought but as essential space for discernment. They leave room on the agenda for prayer and silence, even if that means fewer action items. They review not only what was done, but how it was done, and whether it aligned with God's call. Over time, these rhythms deepen trust. Board members learn how to speak honestly and listen well. They notice when meetings feel rushed or out of alignment. They value the process of decision-making as much as the result. And the congregation feels the difference. A spiritually attentive board does not need to declare its authority. Its presence speaks. Its posture leads. Its faithfulness builds trust that reaches far beyond the boardroom.

Spiritual attentiveness is not about perfection—it is about posture. It is the willingness to return, again and again, to stillness. To recognize when the board has drifted into busyness. To pause when confusion sets in. To breathe before speaking. To pray before deciding. In a culture obsessed with outcomes, it is tempting to equate leadership with relentless motion. But scripture reminds us that the most powerful moments often emerge from stillness. The burning bush. The whisper to Elijah. The watchpost of Habakkuk. The call to Samuel in the night. The words of Christ, inviting us to be still and know. When church boards lead from this place, they offer the congregation something more than good decisions. They offer a living witness to the truth that leadership is not just about getting things done. It is about listening for what God is doing—and then responding with faith, clarity, and courage. Movement leads to stillness. And stillness leads us back to God.

Closing Image

Picture a watchtower at dawn. The world is not yet awake. Below, the camp is quiet. But above, a figure stands—not rushing, not distracted, but present. Watching. Waiting. Listening for the shift in wind, the call in the distance, the whisper of movement on the horizon. That is the posture of spiritual leadership. Not passive. Not panicked. Present. And from that stillness comes clarity. And from that clarity, faithful action.

🕊 Discernment Questions

- Do our meetings create space to listen for the Spirit—or are they filled only with tasks?
- How might a rhythm of reflection strengthen our board's decision-making and relationships?
- When have we felt rushed into action instead of led by discernment?
- What simple practices could help us become more spiritually attentive in our leadership?
- Are we willing to pause, wait, and listen—even when urgency tempts us to move?

Part Three: Protecting What's Sacred

"But test everything; hold fast to what is good."

– 1 Thessalonians 5:21

Part Three: Protecting What's Sacred

This section explores the spiritual meaning of stewardship beyond budgeting or balancing books. We look at money as a sacred trust and budgeting as a tool for honoring what God is doing among us.

- Money as a Spiritual Matter
- The Practice of Faith
- Making the Vision Visible
- Financial Reports that Build Trust
- The Stories We Tell with Our Budget

Chapter 12
Shepherds After My Own Heart

Embracing the protective and pastoral responsibilities of church leadership

"Then I will give you shepherds after my own heart, who will feed you with knowledge and understanding."

– Jeremiah 3:15

A Sacred Trust

There is a profound weight that comes with being entrusted to lead God's people — not a burden, but a call to careful stewardship. In *Jeremiah 3:15*, God promises, *"Then I will give you shepherds after my own heart, who will feed you with knowledge and understanding."* Church leaders are not merely managers or facilitators — they are spiritual shepherds called to protect what is holy, nourish what is growing, and tend to what is vulnerable.

Leadership, in this context, is an act of protection. It is about shielding the church not only from external threats but also from internal decay — the subtle erosion of trust, the quiet misalignment of practices with purpose, or the gradual normalization of behaviors that betray the church's integrity. This chapter explores what it means to lead as a shepherd after God's own heart — not only feeding the flock but guarding the pasture.

Leadership As Protection

The metaphor of the shepherd is not soft. It is courageous. The shepherd does not flee when wolves approach. A true shepherd carries both a staff to guide and a rod to defend. In churches today, this means recognizing the sacred duty of protection — of people, resources, and the church's witness in the world.

This requires:

- **Spiritual Discernment** — a deep awareness of the congregation's spiritual health.
- **Administrative Integrity** — a commitment to policies and procedures that prevent harm.
- **Pastoral Courage** — the willingness to address wrongdoing even when it is uncomfortable.

One of the most insidious dangers churches face is the slow creep of misplaced trust. As Richard Hammar notes, "Many churches refuse to adopt measures that will reduce the risk of embezzlement out of a fear that such measures will reflect a lack of trust" (quoted in *Church Bullies* and *Protecting Your Resources*). But protection is not a sign of mistrust — it is an act of love. It is because we cherish the people and mission of the church that we must put safeguards in place.

Just as shepherds build fences not to imprison sheep but to keep predators out, healthy governance builds boundaries to protect sacred trust. Policies, procedures, and clear lines of accountability are spiritual tools — expressions of love that protect the church's witness and ensure that the energy of the congregation is used in alignment with God's calling. When congregations lack these protections, they often suffer in silence. Financial misconduct, bullying behavior, or theological manipulation can creep in and take root. These are not merely administrative issues; they are spiritual threats that compromise the health and safety of the entire Body. Pastoral leadership must be willing to name what is unhealthy and take faithful action to restore right relationships.

This is not about suspicion. It is about stewardship. Shepherds who care will ask hard questions, implement safeguards, and ensure that systems are designed to protect the vulnerable and hold power accountable. Leaders must pay attention to red flags — financial secrecy, domineering behavior, resistance to accountability, and the normalization of chaos. The presence of one "church bully" who controls the narrative or manipulates decisions can shift an entire culture into fear and paralysis. As seen in *Church Bullies* and *Creating a Healthy Church Governance Culture*, church leaders must remember that enabling unhealthy power dynamics is not compassion — it is abdication.

When God calls someone to be a shepherd, God does not only entrust them with truth and grace — God entrusts them with people. Those people have histories, hurts, and hopes. Shepherds care for the whole flock, not only the loudest sheep. That means creating environments where every voice matters, especially those on the margins. It means practicing transparency, holding one another accountable, and ensuring the church's operations reflect the integrity of the Gospel we proclaim.

The foundation for this kind of leadership is fiduciary responsibility, a term often associated with finance but rooted in deep ethical and spiritual meaning. As outlined in the *Good Governance* and *Ethics in Finance* trainings, fiduciary duty includes the duty of care, duty of loyalty, and duty of obedience. These are not merely legal obligations — they are sacred postures. The duty of care means paying attention, staying informed, and making decisions with diligence. The duty of loyalty means putting the church's mission ahead of personal gain, avoiding conflicts of interest, and refusing to act in self-interest. The duty of obedience means ensuring the church remains faithful to its stated purpose, mission, and ethical practices. These duties are not optional — they are the heartbeat of healthy spiritual leadership.

To lead with these principles requires more than good intentions. It demands structure. Churches must have clear policies and enforce them. The *Policies & Procedures Manual* from Church Training Center emphasizes the importance of following the money and keeping things simple, but also consistent. Procedures for handling offerings, authorizing expenditures, performing reconciliations, and conducting audits should be known, accessible, and actively followed. As shown in *How To Steal From Your Church* and *Maintaining Financial Controls in the Small Ministry*, fraud typically happens not because people are malicious, but because opportunity, need, and rationalization align. Churches must break that triangle by removing opportunity — through dual controls, clear documentation, and regular oversight.

The case examples shared in *Protecting Your Resources* and *Church Embezzlement and How to Prevent It* are sobering reminders of how quickly things can unravel. A trusted treasurer steals tens of thousands. A staff member manipulates rental income. In both cases, the issue was not individual failure alone, but a system that lacked checks and accountability. A shepherd does not only protect the sheep — they build the fence, walk the perimeter, and remain alert for signs of danger.

Church leaders must also guard against emotional and relational harm. In *Church Conflict Resolution* and *Church Board Meetings Focused on God's Calling*, we are reminded that disunity often arises not from theological disagreements but from unclear roles, poor communication, and lack of process. Conflict becomes destructive when leaders are unequipped to handle it or when unhealthy dynamics are allowed to persist unchecked. Shepherds after God's own heart recognize the sacred task of nurturing trust within the leadership body and the wider congregation. They create systems for listening, ensure meetings are structured around mission, and model respect and humility even in disagreement.

Equipping leaders for this level of care includes ongoing training, clear orientation for new board members, and consistent evaluation of the church's culture and systems. The *Creating a Healthy Church Governance Culture* training reminds us that transparency, accountability, and team unity are not aspirational values — they are foundational practices. When boards fail to hold themselves accountable, when financial practices go unreviewed, or when leaders act without clear policy guidance, the congregation suffers. Worse still, the Gospel suffers as trust is eroded and energy is diverted from mission to conflict.

The responsibility of church leadership is not simply to steward money or manage meetings. It is to protect the witness of the church. Every budget, every policy, every agenda reflects what the church values and believes about God, people, and purpose. This is why financial controls are not simply best practices — they are theological commitments. To protect the church's resources is to honor the gifts of the faithful and the mission of the Spirit. To ignore that responsibility is to risk becoming shepherds who feed themselves rather than the flock.

The true shepherd, as Jesus describes in John 10, lays down their life for the sheep. While not all leaders are called to martyrdom, all are called to vigilance, humility, and courage. To be a shepherd after God's own heart is to live in that tension — fierce in protection, gentle in spirit, unwavering in faithfulness. It is to say with our actions what we proclaim with our words: that the people of God are worth protecting, that the mission of God is worth preserving, and that the integrity of the church is a sacred trust we will not abandon.

Closing Image

Picture a shepherd walking the boundary of the pasture at twilight. The sheep are calm. The wind is quiet. But the shepherd keeps watch — not out of fear, but out of love. Every step is a prayer of protection. Every glance a quiet promise: I see you. I will guard you. I will not leave. This is the kind of leadership the church needs — not reactive, but rooted. Not flashy, but faithful. A presence that watches the perimeter, listens for trouble, and stands ready to defend the sacred trust of the flock.

🕊 Discernment Questions

- Where in our church have we tolerated risk out of fear of appearing untrusting?
- What policies or procedures need to be implemented or updated to safeguard our people and our resources?
- Are there any patterns of behavior or power dynamics that need to be lovingly addressed for the sake of the community?
- How does our board model transparency and accountability in ways that build trust with the congregation?
- What systems of oversight are in place — and how are they being actively followed and reviewed?

Chapter 13
The Watchtower and the Shepherd

Understanding fiduciary duty, red flags, and how to intervene when something's not right

"So you, mortal, I have made a sentinel for the house of Israel; whenever you hear a word from my mouth, you shall give them warning from me."

– Ezekiel 33:7

Called to the Watchtower

Church leaders are not only called to shepherd the flock — they are also placed in the watchtower. The sentinel's role is not to dictate but to discern, not to control but to call attention. In *Ezekiel 33:7*, God says, *"I have made you a sentinel… you shall give them warning from me."* The sentinel is not more important than the people — but they are entrusted with visibility. With that visibility comes the responsibility to sound the alarm, even when it is unwelcome.

In today's congregations, that alarm may not come in the form of a prophet's cry but in the quiet signs of misalignment — a treasurer who avoids questions, a volunteer who resists oversight, a pattern of undocumented spending, or a powerful member who seems exempt from accountability. These are not merely administrative concerns. They are spiritual signals. And the church must have leaders willing to notice, to name, and to intervene.

Fiduciary duty is the sacred framework that empowers leaders to stand in the watchtower with clarity and courage. As explored in *Good Governance*, this duty is not just a legal term — it is a theological commitment. To be fiduciaries of the church means to protect what is not ours. It means to make decisions as stewards, not owners. It means to exercise the **duty of care** by being attentive and informed, the **duty of loyalty** by acting without personal agenda, and the **duty of obedience** by ensuring every decision aligns with the mission God has placed before us.

These duties are not passive. They require active engagement, especially when something appears off. *Ethics in Finance* reminds us that board members who serve with good faith, diligence, and ethical awareness are the congregation's first and best protection. This includes not only knowing what the policies are — but being willing to act on them. The failure to question suspicious activity, the reluctance to challenge a dominant personality, or the decision to "let it go" because "they meant well" can all lead to harm. Churches that fail to intervene at the first signs of misalignment risk their credibility, integrity, and future.

The red flags are often subtle at first. As seen in *How To Steal From Your Church* and *Protecting Your Resources*, embezzlement and misuse of funds rarely begin with large thefts. It starts when one person has too much control. When checks go unsigned but still clear. When receipts go missing. When one person prepares, signs, and reconciles accounts. These are not just risky behaviors — they are indicators of systemic vulnerability. It is the responsibility of every board member to know what healthy systems look like, and to raise their voice when something doesn't align.

One of the most dangerous myths in church leadership is the belief that speaking up will cause division. In truth, the refusal to speak up is often what allows division to grow beneath the surface. In *Church Conflict Resolution*, we are reminded that unresolved conflict, especially when tied to money, power, or trust, festers into resentment and disengagement. The role of the sentinel is not to shame or blame, but to serve as a faithful witness — to say, with humility and courage, "Something here deserves our attention."

When boards normalize dysfunction, they silence the Spirit's invitation to accountability. Whether the issue is a charismatic leader circumventing process, a committee member pushing through unapproved expenditures, or a treasurer unwilling to provide reports, these behaviors must be addressed with clarity and compassion. The board has not only the right but the **responsibility** to ask questions, insist on documentation, and pause action until proper review can occur.

Resources such as *Maintaining Financial Controls in the Small Ministry* and *Five Common Mistakes Churches Make With Money* offer practical solutions for intervention. These include implementing vendor acceptance policies, requiring dual signatures, setting limits for discretionary spending, and ensuring separation of duties in all financial processes. But even the best procedures will fail if leaders lack the will to enforce them.

Policies & Procedures from Church Training Center reminds us that clear systems exist to support discernment. Procedures detail the how — policies clarify the why. When leaders hesitate to act because they are unsure whether it's their place, it is the policies that grant permission. And when leaders are tempted to avoid discomfort, it is the sacred trust of fiduciary responsibility that calls them forward.

Standing in the watchtower means remaining attentive even when the landscape looks calm. As *Protecting Your Resources* emphasizes, fraud often goes undetected not because it is well hidden, but because no one is looking. Boards must schedule regular reviews of bank reconciliations, financial reports, and policy compliance — not as a sign of mistrust, but as an act of spiritual stewardship. Healthy organizations normalize oversight as a sign of maturity, not suspicion.

Whistleblowers remain the most common way fraud is discovered in churches, according to the data shared in multiple trainings. External audits catch only a small percentage. This underscores the importance of cultivating a culture where questions are welcomed, feedback is safe, and leaders are not punished for raising concerns. Silence does not protect the church — it exposes it.

For some congregations, the greatest barrier to effective intervention is emotional. Long-term members, beloved leaders, and even ordained ministers may resist oversight, fearing that policies will "get in the way of ministry." But as shared in *Ethics in Finance*, stewardship is not the opposite of faith — it is the embodiment of faith. A well-functioning board reflects the nature of a well-functioning body of Christ: every part working together, honoring its role, and accountable to the whole.

To serve in this way is to reject both apathy and authoritarianism. It is to lead with humility and clarity, remembering always that we are not guarding our own ideas or preferences — we are guarding the sacred. The call is not to micromanage, but to stand watch. To pay attention. To protect what is holy.

Why Some Shepherds Stay Silent

One of the most sobering realities explored across multiple trainings — from *Church Bullies* to *How To Steal From Your Church* — is that even when red flags are visible, church leaders often stay silent. Why? The answer is complex. Sometimes it's fear: of backlash, of relational strain, of being labeled divisive. Other times it's exhaustion: leaders are overwhelmed, unsure of their authority, or unclear on process. And sometimes, it's an ingrained culture of spiritual bypassing — the mistaken belief that being "nice" or "graceful" means ignoring harmful behavior.

But shepherds are not called to ignore the wolves. Nor are they called to maintain appearances at the expense of truth. The watchtower requires clarity. It requires the board to be able to say, "That's not how we operate," and "We need to stop and review this before we move forward." In *Creating a Healthy Church Governance Culture*, we are reminded that healthy boundaries do not stifle the Spirit — they create the conditions where the Spirit can move freely, because the space is safe.

This is why strong board orientation and leadership development are so critical. New board members must not be left to figure it out on their own. They need to know what fiduciary responsibility looks like in practice — and they need the authority, tools, and support to act on it. A policy manual that sits on a shelf serves no one. What's needed is regular training, intentional onboarding, and board cultures that actively normalize accountability.

From Policy to Practice

When procedures are not followed, the door opens to rationalization — not just by those committing wrongdoing, but by those who allow it. *Five Common Mistakes Churches Make With Money* highlights how even simple failures, such as using a preferred vendor without bids, borrowing from restricted funds, or skipping proper approval processes, can escalate into patterns that threaten the integrity of the whole organization. These are not abstract governance issues — they are moments where the watchtower is either staffed or abandoned.

One of the most essential safeguards against this slide is the consistent application of a **Financial Policies & Procedures Manual**, such as the one outlined by Church Training Center. This manual should be reviewed at least annually by the board, updated when necessary, and clearly define roles such as authorizer, preparer, signer, and reconciler. As detailed in *Maintaining Financial Controls in the Small Ministry*, even in small churches with limited volunteers, creative accountability measures — like rotating roles or using an external reviewer — can uphold integrity without overburdening the team.

Churches that fail to document and follow procedures are often those that suffer most when issues arise. The absence of a clear paper trail makes investigation difficult and undermines trust even when no wrongdoing has occurred. Conversely, when a board can demonstrate that controls were followed, decisions were documented, and oversight was intentional, they strengthen not only financial security, but congregational confidence.

The Shepherd's Response to the Warning

When something goes wrong — and it will, at some point — the question is not whether the church failed, but how the church responds. Will leaders respond with defensiveness or humility? With blame or discernment? With secrecy or transparency? The sentinel who sounds the alarm must be met with open ears, not punishment. Boards must build a culture where whistleblowing is seen as an act of care, not betrayal.

In *Church Conflict Resolution*, we are encouraged to confront issues early, before they become crises. This includes early financial warning signs, inappropriate behavior among staff or volunteers, or violations of agreed-upon practices. Addressing concerns in a timely, prayerful, and process-driven way is itself a spiritual discipline. It protects the whole body and models a Gospel-centered way of handling conflict.

The most faithful churches are not those with no problems, but those who are courageous and honest in addressing them. As *Ethics in Finance* reminds us, integrity is not the absence of failure — it is the willingness to respond to failure with repentance, clarity, and change. Shepherds who are "after God's own heart" do not hide from hard truths. They bring them into the light, trusting that healing and renewal are possible.

When a Sentinel Becomes a Shield

There may also come a time when a board member or staff leader sees something deeply concerning — not just a procedural oversight, but an ethical breach, a conflict of interest, or a misuse of funds. In these moments, the shepherd is called not only to observe, but to act. Intervention can take many forms: requesting an internal review, pausing financial activity until questions are resolved, or calling in an outside consultant or auditor. The key is that action must be taken. Silence is not neutral — it becomes complicity.

The *Church Compliance with State and Federal Regulations* and *Church Tax Compliance Workshop* presentations make clear that beyond internal integrity, churches are legally accountable to the state and the IRS. Violations — including mismanagement of restricted funds, excessive benefits to insiders, or lack of reporting — can jeopardize tax-exempt status, lead to penalties, or even result in criminal liability. This is not just about optics. It is about legal and ethical stewardship. Churches must be proactive in understanding their obligations and must ensure that staff and board members alike know what compliance entails.

The challenge is real — and so is the reward. When a congregation takes its fiduciary responsibilities seriously, the culture begins to shift. Trust deepens. Conflicts are addressed early. Resources are used more faithfully. Energy once spent on damage control can now be spent on ministry. This is the harvest of a watchful and wise governing body: a community safeguarded in love and grounded in mission.

A Closing Word From the Watchtower

There is no greater honor than to be entrusted with the care of God's people — and no greater responsibility than to guard the integrity of that trust. The watchtower is not glamorous. It is often quiet. Often costly. It demands alertness, clarity, and the courage to speak when silence would be easier.

But this is sacred work.

As leaders, we are not protecting spreadsheets. We are protecting sacred ground. We are not preserving comfort. We are preserving calling. And we do this not by instinct or fear, but by spiritual attentiveness — by listening for God's guidance in policy, in process, and in each other.

The Spirit does not only guide through silence. Sometimes the Spirit sharpens our vision. Sometimes the Spirit presses us forward. Sometimes the Spirit raises the volume — not to alarm, but to awaken.

When we build systems that are clear, enforce policies that matter, and nurture cultures where accountability is welcomed, we do more than prevent harm. We model the Kingdom. We bear witness to the God who watches over the flock with steadfast love — and calls us to do the same.

Closing Image

Picture a high place overlooking a quiet valley. The village below is peaceful. The fields are still. And yet the sentinel remains at their post—not because something is wrong, but because the role is sacred. To watch. To listen. To be ready. The call to leadership is not always loud. Sometimes it is the quiet resolve to stand watch when no one else notices. Not to guard in fear, but to protect in love. This is what it means to serve in the watchtower—not as a warrior, but as a witness. One who sees with clarity. One who speaks with courage. One who keeps the mission safe.

🕊 Discernment Questions

- How do we create a culture where red flags are named without fear of retaliation?
- What are our procedures for internal investigation, and are they known to the full board?
- Are we unintentionally excusing certain behaviors because of personal loyalty or fear of conflict?
- In what ways are we equipping our leadership to be sentinels — alert, ethical, and courageous?
- What recent decisions have demonstrated our willingness to protect what is sacred, even when it was difficult?

Chapter 14
Keeping the Wolves at Bay

Establishing safeguards, policies, and financial controls to prevent fraud and harm

"See, I am sending you out like sheep into the midst of wolves; so be wise as serpents and innocent as doves."
– Matthew 10:16

"Keep watch over yourselves and over all the flock… I know that after I have gone, savage wolves will come in among you, not sparing the flock."
– Acts 20:28–30

The Quiet Danger Within

Churches are founded on trust — trust in God, in one another, in the power of grace. But scripture reminds us that trust alone is not enough. Jesus sent his disciples into the world with eyes wide open: *"Like sheep in the midst of wolves."* Paul warned the elders of Ephesus that danger would not come only from outside the church — it would rise from within. Harm can enter quietly, through gaps in process, unquestioned habits, or the misuse of authority. The role of church leadership is to guard the flock — not just theologically, but practically.

This chapter is about that sacred responsibility. It is not designed to create suspicion, but to promote wisdom. Over years of working with congregations and judicatory offices, and across a wide range of audits and compliance reviews, the patterns are clear: fraud is preventable. Financial harm is often not the result of a criminal mastermind, but of a system that allowed temptation to grow unchecked.

We will explore the most common vulnerabilities uncovered in church audits, the behaviors that signal deeper risk, and the structures that can prevent devastation. These safeguards are not about fear. They are about faithfulness — protecting the sacred trust we hold on behalf of the people of God.

The Nature of the Wolf

The danger in church leadership is not always dramatic. Rarely does a wolf appear as a villain. More often, harm comes from someone well-loved, long-serving, and overwhelmed. In example after example from our audit files and financial reviews, misconduct started small: a check written without a second signer "just this once," an undocumented reimbursement that "would be approved later," a church credit card used "temporarily." The breach is rarely bold at first — it begins with familiarity and the absence of resistance.

The *Fraud Triangle*, referenced in multiple webinars including *Ethics in Finance* and *Church Embezzlement and How to Prevent It*, names the conditions that give rise to internal misconduct: **pressure, opportunity,** and **rationalization**. A staff member or volunteer facing financial hardship (pressure), with access to funds and no oversight (opportunity), and convinced they'll pay it back or that the church "owes them" for their efforts (rationalization), is in dangerous territory. If leaders are not watching, these small moments accumulate — and what was once unthinkable becomes routine.

Churches are uniquely vulnerable. As emphasized in *Protecting Your Resources* and *Maintaining Financial Controls in the Small Ministry*, many congregations:

- Do not conduct regular internal audits
- Allow one person to count, deposit, and record donations
- Use church credit cards with no review process
- Leave roles and policies undefined
- Fail to train board members on fiduciary duties

None of these practices are malicious — but they are invitations to harm.

Unseen Until It's Too Late

The audit summaries and governance transcripts reveal a consistent and heartbreaking truth: most churches don't realize something is wrong until the damage is extensive. In one reviewed case, a single individual managed all financial records for years, without oversight. The treasurer was trusted, vocal in meetings, and rarely questioned. It wasn't until new leadership came in and asked for basic reports that years of undocumented transfers, missing bank reconciliations, and unexplained expenditures came to light. The congregation was stunned. But the deeper issue wasn't the individual — it was the system that allowed that level of access without accountability.

In another case, a pastoral staff member had been using a ministry debit card to make personal purchases under the guise of program expenses. Because receipts were rarely submitted and monthly statements were never reviewed, thousands of dollars went unnoticed. When the misuse was eventually discovered, the resulting tension caused division in the church and led to leadership resignations. What could have been a simple correction — had policies been in place — instead became a crisis.

Across the board, these situations share three common traits:

1. **Lack of Segregation of Duties**: The same person handles cash, records deposits, and reconciles bank statements.
2. **Absence of Policy Enforcement**: Written policies may exist, but no one is trained to follow them or ensure they are used.
3. **Cultural Resistance to Oversight**: Leaders are hesitant to challenge others, particularly long-serving or ordained individuals, out of fear of conflict.

The results are predictable. And devastating.

Building a Fence Without Breaking Trust

Creating strong financial safeguards does not mean distrusting the people you serve with. It means honoring the sacred nature of the work. As one training in *Five Common Mistakes Churches Make With Money* reminds us, "Policies protect the mission. They protect the people. And they protect the integrity of the Gospel." Just as a shepherd builds a fence not because the sheep are untrustworthy but because the world is unpredictable, the church must establish boundaries that ensure no one carries more authority than is healthy.

Key safeguards that must be implemented — regardless of church size — include:

- **Dual control over all financial transactions**: No one person should prepare, approve, and reconcile the same transaction.
- **Monthly bank reconciliation by someone who does not handle deposits**: A simple yet powerful control that deters fraud.
- **Mandatory submission and review of receipts for all expenditures**: Every credit card transaction, reimbursement, or payment must have documentation reviewed by someone other than the spender.
- **Annual review of all policies and procedures**: Documents must be living tools, not historical artifacts.
- **Regular board training on fiduciary duty and ethical leadership**: New and returning board members must understand their legal and spiritual responsibilities.

The *Policies & Procedures Church Training Center* guide makes a strong case for clear, actionable, and consistently used financial policies. These documents should define:

- Who is authorized to approve spending
- Who may access accounts
- How restricted funds are monitored
- How offerings are counted and deposited
- What to do when a policy is violated

Policies alone do not prevent harm — enforcement does. And enforcement is the work of leadership.

Creating a Culture That Can Say "No"

The greatest safeguard is not a document or a checklist — it is a culture that knows how to say "no." In a healthy governance culture, board members understand that boundaries are a form of care. A strong board does not avoid discomfort; it moves through it with clarity and grace. In *Creating a Healthy Church Governance Culture* and *Church Conflict Resolution*, we are reminded that trust is built through transparency and accountability, not avoidance.

One of the most common vulnerabilities seen in audits and compliance reviews is the concentration of authority in one person — usually someone who "knows how everything works" and has been "doing this for years." When that person resists questions or fails to train others, risk increases. Not because they are necessarily doing something wrong, but because there is no one else who could notice if they were.

A church that learns to say "no" can protect itself from:

- Accepting unclear or improperly restricted donations
- Approving verbal contracts without documentation
- Letting board members operate independently from the body
- Delegating financial authority without checks and balances
- Avoiding conflict by ignoring red flags

Saying "no" to unhealthy practices is how churches say "yes" to integrity. And it must begin at the top. Pastors, treasurers, and board chairs must model this clarity — not only in words but in systems. It is not enough to say "we trust each other." The question is: **Can we demonstrate that trust through our structure?**

When congregations resist oversight or dismiss concerns, they confuse conflict with harm. Raising questions is not divisive. Failing to raise them is.

Responding When Something Isn't Right

Even in the healthiest churches, things can go wrong. A policy may be ignored. An expense may seem suspicious. A report may be missing. What matters most in these moments is how leadership responds. In *Good Governance* and *Ethics in Finance*, it is emphasized that boards must be prepared to act quickly, proportionally, and with spiritual clarity when red flags arise.

When an issue is discovered, the board must:

- **Pause financial activity if needed** to prevent further risk
- **Review the policies and procedures** that apply to the situation
- **Document all findings and steps taken**
- **Bring in outside help if internal resolution is not possible**
- **Communicate with humility and honesty** to those affected

One example from the audit files involved a treasurer who refused to provide documentation for multiple large withdrawals. The board had not seen financial reports in six months. When the chair finally insisted on access, the treasurer resigned — and left behind disorganized records that took a year to reconcile. No clear theft occurred, but the damage to trust and process was severe. The church had no response plan, and the lack of preparation caused even more harm.

Your church should never be caught unprepared. Every board should agree in advance on:

- How suspected misuse of funds will be investigated
- Who has the authority to freeze accounts
- What threshold requires outside consultation or legal counsel
- How the board will communicate findings to the congregation

Transparency is not about exposing people. It's about protecting the church. The point of oversight is not punishment — it's restoration. But restoration requires truth, and truth requires structure.

The Spiritual Cost of Looking Away

Perhaps the most painful discovery across audit after audit is not the dollar amount lost, but the opportunity lost. When misconduct is allowed to fester, even in small ways, the church's spiritual integrity suffers. In *Church Board Meetings Focused on God's Calling*, we are reminded that governance is a form of spiritual leadership. To fail in that role — whether through negligence or avoidance — is to risk the church's ability to respond faithfully to its call.

In one reviewed situation, a volunteer quietly controlled nearly every aspect of the church's finances. Over time, they stopped sharing reports, resisted questions, and became combative when asked to follow new procedures. Board members were aware of the tension but avoided confronting it. After years of dysfunction, the damage was not just financial — it was emotional and spiritual. Leaders had burned out. The congregation had become suspicious. Giving had declined. The mission had stalled.

All of this could have been avoided if someone had spoken up sooner — if someone had been equipped to say, *"This isn't about distrust. It's about being faithful stewards."* The cost of inaction is not measured only in lost funds. It is measured in lost momentum, broken trust, and spiritual fatigue.

To guard the church's finances is to guard its calling. Every dollar entrusted to the church is an expression of faith. Every policy is an act of care. Every time we enforce a boundary, we model a Gospel that values honesty, clarity, and mutual respect. When we fail to protect what is sacred, the impact is felt far beyond the ledger.

Closing Image

Picture a gate at the edge of a pasture. It's not locked out of fear — it's latched with love. Beyond it, the flock grazes peacefully. Within it, trust grows. Leadership doesn't pace the perimeter looking for fault — it watches with faith. Not because harm is expected, but because the Calling is sacred. To build good systems is not to replace trust — it is to embody it. Every clear policy, every safeguarded process, is a quiet act of pastoral care. Not to shame the sheep. But to keep the wolves at bay.

Discernment Questions

- Are there any roles in our church that currently hold too much unchecked authority?
- When was the last time we reviewed our financial policies — and are we actively following them?
- What systems are in place to detect and respond to financial misuse, and do our leaders know how to use them?
- How do we train new board members to understand and live out their fiduciary responsibilities?
- Have we created a culture where raising concerns is encouraged and protected?

Chapter 15
Accountability in Action

Fostering transparency and trust through strong reporting and ethical leadership

"We are making every effort to do what is right, not only in the eyes of the Lord but also in the eyes of others."
– 2 Corinthians 8:21

Stewardship That Can Be Seen

Church leadership is about more than spiritual guidance. It includes the responsibility to handle God's resources with transparency and care. Financial accountability is not just for the treasurer — it belongs to every board member. When we report clearly, ask good questions, and share information openly, we protect trust, empower mission, and witness to our community that the church is a place of integrity.

In this chapter, we will walk through the three most important financial reports used in church life:

1. **Statement of Financial Position** (what we have and owe)
2. **Statement of Activities** (what came in and what went out)
3. **Statement of Cash Flows** (how money moved in real time)

You do not need to be an accountant to understand these. You need only a commitment to learn and a willingness to ask questions.

1. Statement of Financial Position
(Also called a "Balance Sheet" in for-profit businesses)

This report shows the **overall financial health of the church** at a specific point in time. If you've ever looked at a Balance Sheet in a business setting, this is the nonprofit version. It tells you three main things:

- **What the church owns** — this is called **Assets**
- **What the church owes** — this is called **Liabilities**
- **What's left over** — this is called **Equity** (sometimes called Net Assets)

Here's an easy way to understand it:

Think of it like a picture of your personal finances.
Your **assets** are your bank accounts, your car, and your home.
Your **liabilities** are your credit card bills, your mortgage, or anything you still need to pay.
Your **equity** is what you'd have left if you sold everything and paid off your debts.

In the same way, the church's Statement of Financial Position shows **what the church owns, what it owes**, and **what's left** for future ministry.

What to Look for as a Board Member:

You don't need to be a financial expert to read this report faithfully. Here are some basic things to look for:

- **Are the church's assets (what it owns) more than its liabilities (what it owes)?** If so, that's a good sign — the church has a positive net position.
- **Does the church have cash available, or is most of its money tied up in property or long-term investments?** Churches need to have some money on hand for unexpected needs.
- **Are there accounts listed that you don't recognize?** If you see unfamiliar bank accounts, investment accounts, or something labeled "Other Assets," ask questions. No one should feel bad for asking.
- **Are any liabilities unclear?** If there's a loan or bill you don't understand, get clarity. It's part of your role to know what the church is responsible for paying.
- **Is the equity section broken out clearly into General, Restricted, and Designated funds?** These should not be lumped together.
- **Is there a matching asset for each restricted or designated fund?** For example, if a donor gave $10,000 for a new roof, there should be $10,000 sitting in a separate account — not in the general checking account.

- **Current Ratio = Current Assets ÷ Current Liabilities.** This number should be above 1.0. It means the church has enough short-term resources to cover its short-term bills.
- **Liabilities to Equity Ratio = Liabilities ÷ Equity.** This number should stay under 60%. A higher number may mean the church is carrying too much debt.

Why It Matters Spiritually:

This report tells the church, "Are we financially healthy right now?" It's not about how much money we have — it's about whether we're managing what we've been given in a way that allows us to keep saying "yes" to God's call. A strong financial position helps the church move with freedom, not fear. It gives confidence to the congregation and honors the trust of every person who gives.

2. Statement of Activities (Also called the "Profit & Loss Statement" or "Income Statement" in business)

This report shows what money came in and what money went out during a specific time period — usually a month, quarter, or year. It tells the financial story of the church's ministry work during that time. Think of it like your household budget. It shows your income (paycheck, gifts, refunds) and your expenses (groceries, rent, gas), and it tells you if you spent more than you earned or if you came out ahead. In the church, this report usually has three sections: revenue (money received), expenses (money spent), and the bottom line (what's left). The bottom line is either a surplus (more came in than went out) or a deficit (more went out than came in). A surplus is often called "net income" and a deficit is often called "net loss."

What to look for as a board member: First, does the income make sense? Are donations and rental income listed clearly? Is anything missing or labeled in a way that doesn't tell you what it is? Every income line should be understandable. If you don't know what it is, ask. Second, are the expenses in line with the budget you approved? It's okay if some areas go slightly over — life happens — but large overruns or vague expense categories should be explained. Watch for things labeled "miscellaneous" or "other" — if any of those categories are more than $500–1,000, ask what's included. Third, check the personnel line. In most churches, staffing will be the largest expense, and that's normal. The staff are the people doing the work of ministry — preaching, planning, pastoral care, administration, and outreach. If this line is large, it's not a problem — it's a reflection of the people behind the ministry. Finally, check whether restricted and designated funds are reported separately. Restricted income (such as a donation for a specific project) must be tracked and used only for its intended purpose. Designated funds are set aside by the board — and while they're technically unrestricted, the board should still track and honor those designations.

Why it matters spiritually: This report tells the story of how the church used the resources God provided. It's where your ministry priorities show up on paper. It answers questions like: Were we able to do what we felt called to do? Did we use our resources faithfully? Are we stewarding the gifts of the people in ways that reflect our mission? This report isn't just financial — it's theological. It says to the congregation: "Here's how we lived out our calling this season."

3. Statement of Cash Flows (This report is unique to nonprofits and often overlooked — but critically important)

This statement shows how actual money moved in and out of the church during a specific time period. While the Statement of Activities tells you what was earned and spent on paper, the Statement of Cash Flows shows what actually happened with the church's cash. Think of it like tracking the flow of water through a hose — it shows how much came in, how much went out, and what's left in the bucket at the end. This is especially important because sometimes money is received or spent without showing up on the budget yet, and vice versa. This report helps answer the question: Can we pay our bills?

There are three parts to this report: Operating Activities, Investing Activities, and Financing Activities. Operating Activities shows day-to-day cash activity — money received from offerings, rental income, or regular payments, and money spent on salaries, utilities, supplies, etc. This is the most important section for most churches. Investing Activities includes money used to buy or sell long-term items — like a new roof, equipment, or transferring funds into investments. Financing Activities shows loans taken out or repaid.

What to look for as a board member: First, is cash from operations positive? This means the church is bringing in more cash than it is spending on regular ministry. If it's negative, ask why. Is giving down? Were there large unexpected costs? Second, is cash increasing or decreasing overall? If your net income on the Statement of Activities is positive, but your cash is going down, you need to know where the money is going. Third, do the cash balances match what's on your bank statements and Statement of Financial Position? Finally, does this report explain any seasonal trends? For example, many churches receive more income in December and less in the summer — this should be reflected and anticipated in your cash flow.

Why it matters spiritually: Churches do not exist to build savings accounts — but they do need enough cash to carry out their ministry. The Statement of Cash Flows tells leaders whether they are in a position to keep responding to God's call in the coming months. It is a tool of readiness. A church with no cash is a church that may have to delay ministry, defer staff salaries, or cancel important projects. Watching cash flow is not about fear — it's about freedom. It allows the church to say "yes" to the Spirit's invitation with confidence.

4. Report of Restricted and Designated Funds

This is one of the most misunderstood and most important reports a church can produce. While the Statement of Financial Position shows you the total amount of equity, the **Restricted and Designated Funds Report** tells you how much of that equity is spoken for. In simple terms, it answers: "What money do we have that we **can't** spend freely?"

- **Restricted funds** are gifts that donors have limited to a specific use or time. These must only be used in the way the donor instructed — legally and ethically.
- **Designated funds** are amounts the church has chosen to set aside (such as for a building fund, future staff position, or mission trip). These can be changed by the board, but should still be honored unless intentionally redirected.

This report should be updated monthly and include:

- A beginning balance for each fund
- New gifts or transfers in
- Any expenses or transfers out
- An ending balance
- A note identifying where in the church's assets that money is physically held (it should be in a **separate account**, not floating in the general checking account)

What to look for as a board member: Are restricted gifts being used correctly? Is there a trail showing how and when the money was spent? Do the restricted fund balances match what is actually held in separate bank or investment accounts? Are any designated funds still necessary — or should the board consider reallocating them for more urgent needs?

Why it matters spiritually: These are not just "pots of money." They are expressions of trust from the people of God. When someone gives a gift for youth ministry, for future repairs, or to honor a loved one, they are entrusting us with their hope. Managing these funds well is how we honor that hope — and model integrity.

5. Budget Comparisons and Prior-Year Comparisons

Numbers don't mean much without context. That's why churches should never review raw financial reports without comparing them to something — most often, to the **budget** and to **last year's numbers**. These are not separate reports but rather side-by-side columns added to the Statement of Activities.

Budget comparison: This shows how actual revenue and expenses stack up against what the board planned at the beginning of the year. It tells you if you're on track, falling behind, or ahead of expectations.

What to look for: Are we behind in giving compared to the budget? Are we spending more than planned in a particular category? Are there large gaps between the actual and budgeted amounts that need explanation?

Prior-year comparison: This shows how this year's income and expenses compare to the same period last year. It helps you spot trends — positive or negative — and make better decisions going forward.

What to look for: Is giving increasing, decreasing, or holding steady? Are any expenses growing faster than expected? Has a specific ministry area expanded or contracted?

Why it matters spiritually: A budget is a tool of discernment — a way of expressing how we believe God is calling us to use our resources. Comparing our actual numbers to the budget isn't about blame — it's about course correction. If something has changed in the life of the church, the budget may need to change too. These comparisons help the board stay honest and responsive — not to the numbers, but to the reality they represent.

6. Dashboard Reports

Sometimes the best way to see what matters is to **see less** — not by hiding information, but by summarizing it clearly. That's the purpose of a **dashboard report**. Just like the dashboard of a car tells you how fast you're going, how much gas you have, and whether there's a warning light on, a financial dashboard tells church leaders what's happening at a glance.

Every governing body should decide what belongs on their dashboard. There is no one-size-fits-all. It should be tailored to the needs of your church and the comfort level of your leadership team. A dashboard should include key indicators — the numbers that help the board ask: "Are we healthy? Are we sustainable? Are we aligned with our mission?"

Here are common items a church might include:

- **Total cash available** (with comparison to same time last year)
- **Giving to date vs. budgeted giving**
- **Total expenses to date vs. budgeted expenses**
- **Net income or deficit year-to-date**
- **Balance of restricted and designated funds**
- **Cash flow trend over the last three months**
- **Worship attendance or ministry participation** (optional)

Some churches also add a "traffic light" system: green (healthy), yellow (watch), or red (urgent action needed). Others use graphs or color bars to visualize trends.

What to look for as a board member: Does the dashboard give you enough information to know whether a deeper look at the reports is needed? Does it highlight issues in time to respond? Most importantly, does it reflect what the board needs to see in order to govern faithfully?

Why it matters spiritually: Boards don't lead by numbers — they lead by discernment. But discernment requires visibility. The right dashboard isn't a shortcut — it's a **compass**. It keeps the board focused on the big picture so they can make wise decisions in alignment with God's call.

Recommendation: Every board should work with their treasurer or bookkeeper to determine what information they need to see monthly — and then implement a dashboard that fits. This dashboard can grow or shrink as needed, but it should always reflect the information that empowers leadership to act with clarity and confidence.

Bringing It All Together

The work of reviewing financial statements, monitoring restricted funds, comparing budgets, and crafting dashboards is not about creating a well-oiled machine. It is about building a faithful community — one that walks in alignment with the Spirit of God. In a business, the bottom line is profit. In the church, **the bottom line is Calling**.

This cannot be overstated.

When governing bodies forget this, they begin to treat deficits as failure and surpluses as success. But a surplus may indicate missed ministry. A deficit may reveal courage. The point is not whether the numbers are high or low — the point is whether they reflect what the Spirit is calling the church to do.

This is why accountability in the church is different. We are not managing assets for investors. We are stewarding gifts from the people of God for the mission of God. Our task is to **discern the call**, then ask: Are our resources aligned with that call? Is our spending revealing what we say we value? Are we putting our energy, our people, and our dollars where the Spirit is leading?

These are not just financial questions. These are spiritual questions. The board's job is not to protect the budget — it is to protect the mission. And the tools we've outlined in this chapter — statements, comparisons, fund tracking, and dashboards — are not ends in themselves. They are windows. They help us see clearly enough to know if we're walking the path we've been given.

And when the numbers do not align with the calling? Then the job of the governing body is not to retreat, but to return to discernment. To ask what must change. To listen again. To be bold. Because ultimately, our role is not to balance books — it is to follow the voice of the Shepherd.

This is what accountability looks like in the church: not spreadsheets alone, but **Spirit and structure**. Not perfection, but **alignment**. Not fear of failure, but **faithfulness in the work we've been given**.

Closing Image

Picture a lantern in a high window. It casts no judgment. It just shines. Its light is steady, humble, and visible from far off. That's what faithful financial leadership looks like in the church. Not flashy. Not hidden. A light that says: we are stewarding God's resources with care, and we have nothing to conceal. We are not here to impress. We are here to be faithful. And in that faithfulness, trust grows. Mission grows. Integrity becomes not just a value—but a witness.

🕊 Discernment Questions

- Are we evaluating our church like a business — or as a community shaped by God's call?
- When we look at our financial reports, do we see numbers — or ministry?
- Are there areas where our resources and our calling are out of alignment?
- What changes would help us realign our budget, staff, or spending with the Spirit's leading?
- How might our board become more prophetic — asking not only "what can we afford?" but "what is God calling us to do?"

Chapter 16
Subjecting to Governing Authorities

Navigating legal compliance, reporting, and IRS regulations with integrity and faithfulness

"Let every person be subject to the governing authorities; for there is no authority except from God, and those authorities that exist have been instituted by God."
– Romans 13:1

"Remind them to be subject to rulers and authorities, to be obedient, to be ready for every good work."
– Titus 3:1–2

"For the Lord's sake accept the authority of every human institution, whether of the emperor as supreme, or of governors, as sent by him to punish those who do wrong and to praise those who do right. For it is God's will that by doing right you should silence the ignorance of the foolish. As servants of God, live as free people, yet do not use your freedom as a pretext for evil. Honor everyone. Love the family of believers. Fear God. Honor the emperor."

– 1 Peter 2:13-17

Why Compliance Is a Spiritual Matter

Legal compliance is not the most glamorous part of church leadership — but it is one of the most important. Governing a church includes handling finances, reporting to the IRS, following labor laws, and managing tax-exempt status. These are not "side issues." They are essential parts of faithful leadership.

Scripture teaches us to respect civil authority — not out of fear, but out of faith. Being "subject to the governing authorities" doesn't mean obeying blindly. It means living with integrity, fulfilling our obligations, and refusing to take shortcuts. Churches are granted significant legal and financial privileges, including exemption from federal income tax and special tax rules for ministers. But these privileges come with responsibilities — and the board is ultimately accountable.

This chapter offers a practical and spiritual roadmap to the areas your board must understand. We will start with a section that causes confusion for many: ministerial taxes.

1. The Special Tax Status of Ministers

Ministers are treated differently than other employees under federal tax law. This special status reflects the unique nature of pastoral work — and provides several significant tax benefits. It's important to understand these rules so that ministers are protected and the church remains in compliance.

First, **ministers are considered "dual status" employees**. That means they are:

- **Employees** for **federal income tax**
- **Self-employed** for **Social Security and Medicare**

This dual status is not optional — it's required under IRS rules. While it may seem strange, it's designed to balance accountability with the unique freedom of pastoral leadership. Pastors often work outside normal schedules, take on broad responsibilities, and live under unique scrutiny. These tax provisions acknowledge that reality.

Second, ministers are eligible for a **housing allowance**, which allows a portion of their income to be excluded from federal income tax. This is a huge benefit — especially given that many pastors are paid less than professionals with similar education, experience, and responsibilities. The housing allowance can apply to rent, mortgage payments, utilities, and even furnishings — but only if it is properly handled.

Third, ministers are **exempt from FICA** (Social Security and Medicare payroll taxes) — which means the church should **not** withhold those taxes from their paycheck. Instead, ministers pay into Social Security through a separate system called **SECA** (Self-Employment Contributions Act). They must do this when filing their annual tax return, often with quarterly estimated payments.

Let's look closer at how this works — and how your board and treasurer can support it faithfully.

2. Understanding W-2 vs. 1099: Why It Matters

Churches often make the mistake of issuing a 1099 to their pastor or other staff, thinking it's simpler or cheaper. But this is not just incorrect — it can lead to serious IRS penalties. According to federal tax law, pastors are employees of the church for income tax purposes. That means they must receive a **W-2**, not a 1099. The W-2 is the correct form for reporting wages, and it allows the church to comply with its legal responsibilities while also enabling the minister to access certain tax benefits — such as the housing allowance. The 1099 is used only for independent contractors — people who work for themselves, control how the work is done, and are not supervised by the organization. This might include a plumber fixing the boiler or a guest musician who comes once a year — not someone leading the church every week.

Churches that issue a 1099 to their minister are misclassifying the relationship, even if the pastor prefers it. This can result in back taxes, interest, and penalties for both the church and the minister. In short: **if the church directs the work, provides a space, and has ongoing authority — it's a W-2 situation.** This applies even if the person is part-time or considered "contract" internally. The IRS looks at the function, not the title. The church is responsible for issuing W-2s by January 31 each year, even if no income tax is withheld. Ministers are considered self-employed for Social Security and Medicare — so they are responsible for paying those taxes directly using SECA when filing their own tax returns.

This is where FICA and SECA get confusing for many church boards. Most employees have FICA taxes withheld from their pay — 6.2% for Social Security and 1.45% for Medicare, with the employer matching those amounts. But ministers don't have FICA withheld. Instead, they pay both halves (a total of 15.3%) under SECA when they file their tax return. This tax is real, and it must be planned for. The church **must not** withhold or pay FICA for a minister, because doing so could **jeopardize the housing allowance** and create IRS problems. However, the church **can** help ministers plan by encouraging quarterly estimated payments or by offering a Social Security offset — a taxable benefit designed to help cover this cost.

The bottom line: if the minister is being paid by the church, issue a W-2, do not withhold FICA, and understand that the minister is self-employed for Social Security and Medicare. It's not intuitive, but it's the law — and honoring it helps everyone stay in good standing.

3. Housing Allowance: One of the Most Valuable Benefits for Ministers

The housing allowance is one of the most significant tax benefits available to clergy — and one of the most commonly mishandled. When properly designated, the housing allowance allows a portion of the minister's pay to be excluded from federal income tax. This can result in thousands of dollars in savings each year. But it only works if the church follows the rules carefully.

First, the housing allowance must be **approved in advance** — it cannot be applied retroactively. That means if your board waits until February to designate the allowance, the pastor cannot apply it to January's pay. The IRS is strict about this. The housing allowance must be set **before** the pay is issued, and should be included in board minutes or a formal employment agreement. If it's not documented ahead of time, it doesn't count.

Second, the amount designated must be **reasonable** and tied to actual housing costs — including rent or mortgage, utilities, furnishings, maintenance, and other eligible expenses. The IRS will only allow the minister to exclude the **lowest** of three things: the amount designated by the church, the amount actually spent on housing, or the fair rental value of the home including furnishings and utilities. That means churches should not just designate "everything" — they should work with the minister to estimate a realistic amount each year.

Third, mid-year changes are allowed — but only for the remaining portion of the year. If a pastor moves, experiences a change in housing costs, or needs to adjust the amount, the board can update the designation going forward. But again, **it cannot apply retroactively**. Only future pay periods can be covered by a new designation.

Boards should also be aware that the housing allowance is **excluded from federal income tax**, but **not** from SECA. Ministers still pay self-employment taxes on the value of the housing allowance — and this is often misunderstood. It's one more reason why ministers need support and education around quarterly tax planning.

Your board should vote to approve the housing allowance **annually**, ideally before January 1, and always record the amount in the board minutes. This one simple step can provide your minister with a significant and deserved financial benefit — while also demonstrating the church's care and attention to legal detail.

4. Payroll and Withholding: Getting It Right Protects the Church and Its Staff

Churches that have employees — including pastors, administrative staff, custodians, and musicians — are responsible for all standard employer duties under the law. This includes properly calculating, withholding, and depositing income taxes (except for ministers), as well as preparing and submitting payroll reports. Most churches file IRS Form 941 quarterly to report wages paid and federal taxes withheld. Smaller churches may be allowed to file Form 944 annually, but only if the IRS has specifically notified them. Failure to file these forms or deposit taxes on time can lead to steep penalties, even if the amounts are small.

The church is also required to issue **Form W-2** to every employee by **January 31** each year. This includes reporting the total wages, any federal and state income taxes withheld, and additional items such as housing allowance in **Box 14** for ministers. If the church offers a **Social Security offset** (an additional amount to help the minister pay SECA taxes), this must be included in Box 1 as taxable income. All W-2s must be submitted to the Social Security Administration along with a **W-3 summary form**, and the church must retain copies for its records.

One common mistake is assuming that if the church isn't withholding taxes, it doesn't need to issue a W-2. This is incorrect. **Even if no taxes are withheld, a W-2 must still be issued** — especially for ministers. Not doing so places the minister in a difficult position and places the church at legal risk. If someone is working under the church's supervision and direction, they are almost certainly an employee. That means payroll must be handled accordingly.

Using a payroll service can be extremely helpful, but it does not remove the board's responsibility. The IRS holds the employer —

not the payroll provider — legally accountable for mistakes. So if you outsource payroll, ensure that the provider understands the special rules around clergy compensation, housing allowance, and SECA vs. FICA. Review every W-2 before it's issued. Ask for reports that compare quarterly Form 941s to W-2 totals to confirm they match. Retain all documentation for at least four years in case of audit.

Good payroll practices are not just legal requirements. They are a form of hospitality. They say to your staff, "We take your livelihood seriously." It's a way of honoring those who serve the church and showing that the church itself is trustworthy in matters both sacred and administrative.

5. Independent Contractors and 1099s: Use With Caution

Not everyone the church pays is an employee — but that doesn't mean they should automatically receive a 1099. Independent contractors are people who provide services to the church but are not under the church's direction or control. They typically set their own schedule, provide their own tools, and do similar work for multiple clients. Examples might include a piano tuner, a guest speaker who is not regularly scheduled, or a web developer who works remotely for a few weeks to build the church's new site.

However, it's critical to understand that **most recurring, supervised, or directed roles should be classified as employees — not contractors.** If the church decides what will be done, when, and how, the person is likely an employee and must receive a W-2. Issuing a 1099 to someone who should be on payroll is a legal violation that can lead to penalties for both unpaid taxes and misclassification.

Some states — like **California and Illinois** — apply the **ABC Test**, which makes it very difficult to classify someone as an independent contractor. While these states are frequently referenced due to their clarity and enforcement, the rules vary widely across the U.S. That's why every church must **research**

their own state's rules or consult a professional to ensure they're in compliance. What's acceptable in one state may be prohibited in another.

If a person is properly classified as a contractor, the church must issue **Form 1099-NEC** (not 1099-MISC) if that person was paid $600 or more during the year. This includes solo musicians, graphic designers, or substitute custodians — as long as they meet the contractor criteria. The church must also submit **Form 1096** to the IRS summarizing all 1099s issued, and this too is due by **January 31** each year.

To stay compliant, your board should ensure that:

- W-9 forms are collected from all contractors before issuing payment
- Each working relationship is reviewed to determine proper classification
- Contractor payments are tracked throughout the year to avoid surprises
- The treasurer or bookkeeper files all necessary forms by the January deadline

This attention to detail is not just about compliance — it reflects the church's values. Fair treatment of those we hire, whether full-time staff or part-time contractors, is a form of justice. It shows that the church values the labor of all people and seeks to operate with integrity in every transaction.

6. Housing Allowance: Common Mistakes and How to Avoid Them

The housing allowance is one of the most important benefits the church can offer its minister — and one of the most frequently misunderstood. Done properly, it allows the minister to exclude a portion of their pay from **federal income tax** (though not SECA), significantly reducing their tax burden. Done incorrectly, it offers no benefit at all and may cause the minister to owe back taxes with interest.

To be valid, a housing allowance must meet the following conditions:

- **It must be approved in advance** by the governing body or appropriate authority.
- **It must be documented in writing** — usually in the board minutes or in a formal employment agreement.
- **It must be designated before the payment is made.** You cannot apply a housing allowance retroactively. Once a paycheck has been issued, it is too late to designate any portion of it as housing allowance.

This is a critical detail: many churches forget to act before the new year and then try to "fix it" in March. Unfortunately, the IRS does not allow retroactive designations. If you miss the deadline, those months are lost — and the pastor will owe tax on the full amount.

Mid-year changes are allowed, but only for the remaining months of the year. For example, if a pastor moves to a more expensive home in July, the board can vote to increase the housing allowance for August through December. However, they still cannot change what was already paid in January through July.

A good practice is for the board to designate the housing allowance **annually**, in November or December, so that it is in place for January 1. The designated amount should be realistic, based on what the minister expects to spend on housing, and supported by a worksheet or estimate. Churches should remember that the IRS will only allow the minister to exclude the **lowest** of (1) the amount designated, (2) the amount actually spent, or (3) the fair rental value of the home, including furnishings and utilities. Over-designating won't help — it only sets up confusion later.

Finally, the housing allowance must be **reported properly**. It is not included in **Box 1** of the W-2, but should be clearly noted in **Box**

14 or in a separate letter to the minister. It is not subject to federal income tax, but it **is subject to SECA** — so the minister must include it when calculating their self-employment tax.

Your board doesn't need to become tax experts — but it does need to act with clarity and consistency. Approving a housing allowance is one of the most direct ways the church can support its minister's well-being. Doing it right is an act of stewardship and pastoral care. Doing it wrong can cause harm, stress, and unnecessary financial burden for someone already carrying the weight of spiritual leadership.

7. Unrelated Business Income: When Church Revenue Becomes Taxable

Most church income — such as tithes, offerings, and donations — is not taxable because it directly supports the church's religious mission. However, if a church earns income from activities that are **not related to its core ministry**, that income may be subject to tax under the rules for **Unrelated Business Income Tax (UBIT)**.

UBIT exists to prevent tax-exempt organizations from competing unfairly with for-profit businesses. The IRS defines unrelated business income as money earned from an activity that meets all three of the following criteria:

- It is a **trade or business** (something done to make money)
- It is **regularly carried on** (not just once a year or occasionally)
- It is **not substantially related** to the church's tax-exempt purpose

Examples include:

- Renting out your parking lot on weekdays to local commuters
- Selling advertising space in your bulletin or newsletter

- Operating a church café or bookstore that is open to the public and not staffed by volunteers
- Hosting a thrift store where most items are purchased (not donated) and resold for profit

Exceptions exist. Even if the income meets the criteria above, it is not taxable if:

- Substantially all the work is done by volunteers
- The activity exists mainly for the convenience of members
- The goods sold are mostly donated

In most cases, **rental income** from church property is not taxable. However, if the property was purchased with borrowed funds and is not used primarily for ministry, the income might become taxable under "debt-financed property" rules. This is where a seemingly innocent lease agreement can have serious tax implications.

If your church has unrelated business income totaling more than $1,000 in a year, you must file **IRS Form 990-T** and pay tax on the profit at regular corporate tax rates. If you're not sure whether an activity qualifies, **ask before you act**. It's better to report it properly than to risk a penalty or loss of tax-exempt status.

Your board should be aware of all income sources and ask:

- Does this activity support our religious purpose?
- Who is doing the work — staff, volunteers, or a paid manager?
- Is this a one-time fundraiser or an ongoing business?
- Do we need to report and pay taxes on it?

Churches don't need to fear UBIT, but they do need to understand it. It's not about punishment — it's about fairness. Churches are not businesses, but when they act like businesses, they may be taxed like them. Knowing the boundaries helps protect your ministry and keeps the church focused on what matters most.

8. Charitable Contributions: Protecting Donors and Honoring Their Intent

Churches depend on the generosity of their members and supporters. These contributions are not only sacred acts of worship — they are also tax-deductible gifts under IRS rules. But that tax-deductibility comes with legal expectations. Churches are required to follow specific guidelines for acknowledging contributions, especially when donors intend to claim those gifts on their tax returns.

The IRS places the burden of documentation on the **donor**, not the church. But if the church fails to provide proper receipts or acknowledgments, the donor may be unable to deduct their gift — and trust can be lost. The church's role is to assist in good faith by offering timely, accurate records and maintaining transparency.

What your church should do:

- Provide annual contribution statements to donors by **January 31**, detailing the total amount given and listing any individual gifts of $250 or more.
- For any single contribution of **$250 or more**, provide a **written acknowledgment** that includes the donor's name, the amount given, the date, and a statement confirming whether any goods or services were provided in return.
- If the donor received something of value in return (like a dinner or event ticket), the church must provide a **good faith estimate** of the value of those goods or services.
- For **quid pro quo** contributions (where part of the donation is for goods or services), the church must notify the donor of the deductible portion — for example, "You donated $100 for the banquet. The value of the meal was $40, so your deductible contribution is $60."
- Keep clear records of all donations, including the date received, amount, donor name, and any notes about restrictions or designations.

Churches are **not required to assign a value to non-cash gifts**, such as furniture or equipment. However, the church should acknowledge the gift in writing with a description of the item and a statement confirming whether any goods or services were provided in return.

Designated vs. Restricted Gifts: Some gifts come with donor instructions — for example, "This is for the youth retreat." These are **restricted funds** and must be used only for the stated purpose. If the church cannot honor the request, it must either return the gift or get the donor's written permission to reallocate it. Other gifts are designated internally by the board (e.g., "building reserve") — these can be changed by board vote. Both must be tracked with care, but donor restrictions are legally binding.

Spiritual framing: Receiving a gift is an act of trust. When someone gives to the church, they are placing part of their story in our hands. We must receive it with reverence, record it with care, and use it as intended. Financial integrity is not just about avoiding trouble — it's about honoring the faithfulness of the people of God. When churches take contribution reporting seriously, they are saying to every giver: "Your gift matters. And we will treat it that way."

9. Gift Acceptance Policies: Clarity Before the Crisis

While most church gifts come in the form of cash, checks, or online donations, there will be times when a member offers a non-cash gift — a vehicle, a timeshare, a piece of art, or even property. These can be blessings. But they can also become burdens — especially if there are hidden costs, legal complications, or strings attached. That's why every church should have a **Gift Acceptance Policy**.

A Gift Acceptance Policy is a written set of guidelines that helps the church evaluate whether to receive a particular gift — and how to handle it once it's accepted. It is **not** a sign of greed or suspicion. It's a sign of stewardship. It says to the congregation: "We are committed to using your gifts wisely — and we'll be clear about what we can and cannot accept."

Here's what a good policy might include:

- **Who decides?** Designate a team (e.g., the finance committee, trustees, or a designated review group) that has the authority to accept or decline unusual gifts.
- **What types of gifts need review?** Most policies specify that **non-cash gifts, real estate, closely held stock, vehicles,** and **donor-directed gifts** must be reviewed before being accepted.
- **What factors will be considered?** These may include potential costs (like insurance or maintenance), resale difficulty, potential liability, or conflicts with the church's mission or values.
- **When can a gift be declined?** The church must reserve the right to graciously decline gifts that come with unreasonable conditions, excessive risk, or costs that outweigh the value.
- **What happens after a gift is accepted?** The policy should include clear steps for documentation, IRS compliance, and donor communication.

For example, if someone offers the church a used RV for youth ministry, the board should ask: Do we have insurance? Will we use it? Can we store it? Would it cost more to keep than to sell? Is the donor expecting a certain kind of recognition or ongoing control? Without a policy in place, the church may feel pressure to say yes when wisdom says wait.

It's also important to understand the IRS rules about non-cash gifts. If the church receives a non-cash gift valued at more than $5,000 and sells it within three years, it may need to file **IRS Form 8282**. The donor, in turn, may need **Form 8283** to claim a deduction — and in most cases, the church is **not** responsible for appraising the gift's value.

Why it matters spiritually: Saying yes to a gift should never distract the church from its mission. And saying no should never damage a relationship. A Gift Acceptance Policy gives you language and clarity **before** the emotion and urgency of a specific situation arise. It helps avoid awkward conversations and protect the church from being pulled into arrangements that are not sustainable.

In summary: a Gift Acceptance Policy is about freedom. It frees the church to say yes with joy and no with grace — keeping the focus on stewardship, not entanglement. It is one more way governing bodies honor their calling to safeguard what is sacred.

10. Recordkeeping and Retention: Faithfulness in the Folders

Every church, no matter its size, must maintain proper records. Good recordkeeping is not just about audits or tax forms — it's about being able to tell the story of how the church has stewarded its resources over time. It shows continuity through leadership transitions, helps new board members understand the church's operations, and builds trust with donors, auditors, and the wider community.

The IRS and many state agencies have clear expectations about what must be kept — and for how long. But even beyond legal requirements, the church should view recordkeeping as part of its spiritual integrity. We don't just document for the government; we document for the sake of accountability, memory, and wisdom.

Here's a basic guide for what to retain — and how long to retain it:

- **Contribution records**: Keep donation records and acknowledgment letters for at least 7 years.
- **Payroll records**: Retain W-2s, 941s, salary agreements, and housing allowance approvals for at least 4 years after the year in which taxes were filed.

- **Corporate records**: Keep articles of incorporation, bylaws, board minutes, and policies (including Gift Acceptance and Conflict of Interest Policies) permanently.
- **Tax-exemption documents**: Keep all IRS determination letters, correspondence, and related filings permanently.
- **Property records**: Keep deeds, mortgage information, and documentation of capital improvements for at least 4 years after the property is sold or retired.
- **Expense receipts and bank statements**: Retain for a minimum of 3–4 years, longer if related to grants or designated funds.

Records should be stored securely — but accessible. At least one copy of critical documents should be kept in a fire-safe or scanned to a secure cloud storage account. Passwords for financial systems, donor software, and payroll portals should be known by more than one authorized person and updated when leadership changes.

Tip for boards: At the beginning of each year, ask: Who is reviewing our records? Do we have what we need from last year? Is anything missing? Can someone new step in and find what they need without confusion? Good records protect not only the church — they protect the people who serve it.

Spiritual framing: Keeping accurate, well-organized records is a way of saying, "We remember. We are accountable. We honor the gifts and work that came before us." It's a sacred form of stewardship — not for its own sake, but so that the next generation can build with confidence on a foundation of trust.

11. State and Local Compliance: Knowing Your Context

While federal tax law applies to all churches in the United States, each **state has its own rules** about how churches operate legally within its borders. Some states require churches to file annual or biennial reports to maintain their nonprofit status. Others impose rules about property tax exemptions, sales tax collection, or unemployment insurance. It is not safe to assume that what is true in one state applies everywhere. Your board must take responsibility for understanding and following the laws of your specific state.

For example, in **California** and **Illinois**, churches must register with the state's tax authorities to receive state tax-exempt status. This is **separate** from the church's federal exemption through the IRS. In both states, churches must also file a "Statement of Information" or similar report every year or two with the Secretary of State. If these filings are missed, the church may be **suspended** or **administratively dissolved** — even if everything is fine with the IRS.

In many states, **property tax exemption** is not automatic. Churches must apply for exemption and may need to reapply if they expand or change the use of their property. Vacant land, rented buildings, or non-ministry spaces (like parking lots used for public purposes) may not be fully exempt. Similarly, most states **do not exempt churches from paying sales tax** on purchases. If your church operates a bookstore or sells merchandise, you may need to collect and remit sales tax — depending on the state's rules.

Churches are often exempt from **unemployment insurance taxes**, but not always. In some states, if a church operates a preschool, food pantry, or other social service program, it may be required to participate in the state's unemployment system. This is especially important if you have employees outside of traditional ministry roles.

Your board's responsibility is to ask:

- Are we properly registered with our state?
- Are we in good standing with the Secretary of State or state tax authority?
- Have we filed all required reports this year?
- Do we know the rules for sales tax, property tax, and unemployment in our state?

If you don't know, ask. Contact your Secretary of State's office, Department of Revenue, or a nonprofit legal clinic. Many states offer free guides for exempt organizations. And if you're not sure what's required — especially for programs outside traditional worship — don't guess. **Research. Ask. Confirm.** Faithfulness includes knowing the laws where we serve.

Spiritual framing: Jesus taught that we are to "render to Caesar what is Caesar's" — not with resentment, but with clarity. When the church fulfills its obligations to local authorities, it strengthens its witness. It says, "We are not hiding. We are present, honest, and committed to the common good." Being rooted in place means knowing what the place requires — and meeting those requirements as a matter of integrity.

Bringing It All Together: Compliance as a Form of Discipleship

Compliance is not just paperwork. It is a form of discipleship. It is how we care for the structures that carry the message. It is how we honor the labor of our ministers and staff, how we protect the integrity of our witness, and how we ensure that every gift given in faith is stewarded with faithfulness.

Governing bodies are not called to be tax experts. But they are called to **care**. To ask the right questions. To seek help when needed. To ensure that what happens behind the scenes reflects the same trust and clarity that we preach from the pulpit.

When we file the right forms, classify workers properly, designate housing allowances in time, and honor the intentions of our donors — we are not just "checking boxes." We are demonstrating that the church is worthy of trust. That we value the people who serve. That we are paying attention to the sacred and the simple alike.

When we say "yes" to accountability and "no" to shortcuts, we protect the mission. We keep the church free to say yes to the Spirit — not bound up in legal confusion or reactive crisis. We avoid the pain of penalties, audits, or reputational harm. We create systems that allow the church to thrive, not just survive.

And when we don't know something? We ask. We learn. We grow. Because integrity doesn't mean having all the answers. It means being willing to seek them. That is the true call of a governing body: not just to lead, but to lead **faithfully**.

Closing Image

Picture a ledger—not dusty or hidden away, but open, organized, and well-kept. Next to it sits a candle, its flame steady, casting light over names, figures, and signatures. This is not bureaucracy. This is stewardship. Every entry says: we are paying attention. Every form filed on time says: we are trustworthy. Every question asked says: we are learners. The church does not need to fear the law when it walks in the light. When its books are open and its hands are clean, the church becomes what it was always called to be: a witness. Not just in worship—but in how it honors what is required.

🕊 Discernment Questions

- Are we clear about our legal obligations as a board?
- What areas of compliance have we avoided out of confusion or fear?
- Do we have policies in place to protect our staff, our funds, and our tax-exempt status?
- Have we documented our housing allowance designations, staff classifications, and charitable gift procedures properly?
- What steps can we take this month to strengthen our systems and seek outside help where needed?

Part Four: Resourcing the Vision

"Bring the full tithe into the storehouse... and see if I will not open the windows of heaven for you and pour down for you an overflowing blessing."

– Malachi 3:10

Part Four: Resourcing the Vision

This section equips leaders to plan with purpose, align resources with the church's unique calling, and respond with integrity to opportunities, challenges, and financial decisions that shape the future.

- Plans Committed in Prayer
- Written on Our Hearts
- The Measure You Give
- Threads to Refuse

Chapter 17
Plans Committed in Prayer

Aligning the financial planning process with discernment and mission

"Commit your work to the Lord, and your plans will be established."
– Proverbs 16:3

Budgeting is not simply an administrative requirement — it is a spiritual act of trust. The church does not plan like a business, projecting quarterly profits or protecting market share. We plan by listening. We plan by asking: *What is God calling us to do in this season?* And then we build a plan that reflects that calling — with courage, honesty, and faith.

When we commit our work to God, as Proverbs 16:3 reminds us, we do not merely ask God to bless what we've already decided. We open the planning process itself to transformation. We let go of familiar line items and inherited assumptions. We let go of our fear that there won't be enough. We even let go of our need for control. This is what it means to *commit our plans in prayer* — to surrender the process before the product ever appears.

Every budget is a living story. It testifies to what we value, what we hope for, and how we believe God is moving among us. In this sense, the governing body becomes not only the steward of resources, but the spiritual author of a collective response.

Too many churches begin their planning with the previous year's budget. They review what they spent, add a little here, subtract a little there, and call it discernment. But when the process starts with numbers instead of purpose, it is nearly impossible to create a budget that inspires.

The foundation of faithful budgeting is *alignment with Calling*. This means asking questions that cannot be answered by financial reports alone:

- Where is the Spirit leading us this year?
- What must we release in order to respond fully?
- What ministries need to be born — or gracefully retired?

When we start here — with God's invitation — the numbers take on meaning. We no longer see them as constraints, but as tools. We no longer treat the budget like a chore, but as a chance to say yes to God's next chapter for our church.

And we do not take this journey alone. A healthy budget process invites wide participation. Finance teams, ministry leads, pastors, and congregants each offer essential insight. The role of the governing body is to listen well, communicate clearly, and hold the vision at the center — even when trade-offs are required.

A faithful budget process begins by setting the stage well in advance. Churches that struggle with budgeting often wait too long to begin, compress decision-making into a single meeting, or fail to involve the right voices at the right time. Good stewardship requires good structure — and structure requires time.

Begin with the end in mind. When will the congregation be asked to vote on the budget? Count backward from that date, allowing time for revisions, approvals, and presentations. Build in margin. Aim not just to finish on time, but to create space for prayerful reflection, transparent dialogue, and honest evaluation. This is not just a financial practice — it is a spiritual discipline.

The timeline for budget development typically includes:

- Requests from committees and ministries
- Review by staff and financial leadership
- Initial draft by the finance team or treasurer
- Review and revision by the governing body
- Final presentation to the congregation

Each step offers an opportunity to shape the narrative — not just the numbers. The role of the governing body is to ensure that the process is spiritually grounded, structurally sound, and accessible to the whole church. This means honoring deadlines, yes — but also fostering trust.

Communication is key. When leaders fail to communicate budget decisions clearly, suspicion grows. When there are financial challenges, congregants must hear that with honesty and hope. When there are ministry dreams, those dreams must be shared with joy and courage. A budget may be a set of numbers — but it is also a story. And stories need storytellers.

A spiritually grounded budget process avoids common pitfalls:

- *Confusing presentations*: No unexplained numbers, acronyms, or insider language
- *Hidden agendas*: Transparency is a form of trust
- *Silencing voices*: Invite feedback early and often
- *Unreasonable expectations*: Budgets must be both faithful and realistic

Churches that commit their plans in prayer — and to one another — will find that even hard decisions can be held with grace.

Churches that commit their plans in prayer — and to one another — will find that even hard decisions can be held with grace. But grace is not passive. It requires clarity. It requires process. And it requires courage.

A critical aspect of faith-filled budgeting is determining *how* decisions will be made — and by *whom*. Do your bylaws require budget approval by the Finance Committee? The Church Council? The entire congregation? Can the governing body revise the budget midyear? These questions should never be afterthoughts. When authority is unclear or unexamined, it becomes a breeding ground for frustration or mistrust. Part of the governing body's sacred work is to ensure that decisions are made with integrity, in the light of day, and according to the structures the church has prayerfully adopted.

And yet, faithful budgeting is more than a procedural checklist. It is a spiritual discernment of what must begin, what must end, and what must be held in trust for the future. This is where tools like *zero-based budgeting* become more than financial strategies — they become acts of theological courage.

Zero-based budgeting asks: *If we weren't already doing this, would we start it now?* It invites us to strip away assumptions and look freshly at each expense. Not all churches can fully implement this model every year — but every church can adopt its spirit. What ministries are receiving funds because they have always been there, not because they reflect who we are today? What expenses might be legacy lines, once meaningful, now unloved?

Alongside zero-based thinking, churches should also review **trends**. Not because the past dictates the future — but because it helps reveal patterns. What expenses are increasing faster than anticipated? What income sources have been more faithful than expected? What financial surprises became spiritual stories?

When the budget begins to take shape, the focus shifts from discernment to **presentation** — and this, too, is sacred work. Budgets are often presented in language that alienates: spreadsheets filled with abbreviations, technical categories, or opaque formulas. But the story behind the budget matters far more than the format. A faithful budget presentation tells a story of God's call and the community's response.

This means linking numbers to mission. Don't just say how much is allocated to youth ministry — remind the church what transformation happens there. Don't just show a number under "Outreach" — tell the story of the family fed, the neighbor welcomed, the heart healed. Budgets become compelling when they connect to what matters. This is not emotional manipulation. It is honest testimony.

Visuals matter, too. Clear printouts. Legible fonts. Pie charts that illuminate rather than confuse. Breakdowns by ministry, not just category. Every act of clarity is an act of hospitality — and hospitality is a ministry.

This kind of presentation also prepares the congregation for generosity. Stewardship and budgeting must never be disconnected. The more the church understands what their giving supports —

and how their giving fuels the call of God among them — the more empowered and joyful their response becomes. A disconnected budget presentation can flatten even the most inspiring stewardship campaign. But a well-integrated budget, rooted in story and Spirit, becomes a powerful invitation.

Of course, not every season feels abundant. Sometimes governing bodies are called to make painful cuts. Sometimes beloved ministries must pause. Sometimes the call of God requires a budget that steps into risk. In these moments, it is tempting to panic — or to freeze. But churches led by faith rather than fear remember this truth: *God is still at work in the wilderness.*

In seasons of financial challenge, the role of the governing body is not to fix everything, but to be honest about what is — and faithful about what could be. Some line items may shrink, but the Spirit has not. Some dreams may be delayed, but the church's call remains. Lean seasons invite creativity, deepen reliance, and clarify what truly matters.

In every season, the church is called to plan not as a business, but as a body. A body that listens. A body that serves. A body that remembers that all we have has been entrusted by God — and all we do is a response to that grace.

༃ Discernment Questions

- How often do we stop and pray during our financial decision-making?
- What role does Calling play in our budget conversations?
- Are our financial goals shaped by faith or by fear?
- Have we confused efficiency with spiritual wisdom in our planning process?
- How can we make room for Spirit-led surprises in our fiscal year?

Chapter 18
Written On Our Hearts

Presenting budgets as living testimony of what God is doing among us

"You yourselves are our letter, written on our hearts, known and read by everyone. You show that you are a letter from Christ… written not with ink but with the Spirit of the living God, not on tablets of stone but on tablets of human hearts."
– 2 Corinthians 3:2–3

A church's budget is not just a financial document. It is a letter. It tells a story — not merely of dollars allocated, but of lives transformed. When the governing body presents the annual budget to the congregation, they are not simply making the case for funding. They are bearing witness to what God is doing among them.

Too often, church budgets are introduced with a sigh, printed with small fonts, read aloud with hesitation, and received with glazed eyes. But it doesn't have to be that way. If we believe the church exists to carry out the work of Christ in the world, then every financial plan is part of the gospel story — because it reveals how we are responding to the call of God in our time and place.

A faithful budget presentation must speak to the heart, not just the head. It must inspire vision, not just explain logistics. It must connect people to one another, not separate those "in the know" from those just trying to keep up. This is not manipulation. It is ministry. And the governing body, by embracing this role, becomes not only stewards of money — but stewards of hope.

Presenting a budget well begins long before the day of the meeting. It begins with how we think about the budget itself. Is it just a financial formality — or a living testimony? Do we approach it as a series of constraints — or a witness to God's abundance? Do we treat it as an obligation — or an invitation?

Budgets written in love can be presented with love. Budgets shaped by discernment can be shared with joy. And when a congregation hears its own heartbeat in the presentation, the response is not just financial — it is spiritual.

To present a budget as a living testimony, we must first reimagine how we frame it. Numbers by themselves do not inspire. Stories do. When people hear how a meal ministry brought comfort to a grieving neighbor, how a youth retreat sparked new faith, or how worship lifted someone from despair — they don't just learn *what* the church is doing, they feel *why* it matters.

The governing body's role is to bring those stories to the surface. Instead of leading with categories and totals, lead with meaning. Connect the line item to the life it touches. Every number in the budget should answer the deeper question: *What does this make possible?* When the church sees the connection between their giving and their calling, generosity becomes a natural response.

This means shifting from technical reporting to spiritual storytelling. It means designing a presentation that engages the heart — using testimonies, images, even music when appropriate. It means giving people a glimpse of what God is doing, and how their gifts are part of that sacred work.

A line item for "Children's Ministry" becomes powerful when accompanied by a story about a child who found belonging for the first time. A section on "Community Outreach" takes on new meaning when paired with a photo from the food pantry or a note from someone who was helped. Even general expenses like utilities and staffing can be reframed as the invisible scaffolding that holds ministry together.

The budget becomes more than a tool for accountability — it becomes a tool for connection.

The most effective budget presentations are not polished performances — they are honest, heartfelt conversations. They reflect both the church's hopes and its limitations. They acknowledge the challenges while inviting the congregation into the joy of shared responsibility. The role of the governing body is not to convince, but to *connect* — to help people see themselves as co-authors in the church's unfolding story.

This kind of presentation begins with preparation. The governing body must ensure that the presentation is clear, accessible, and rooted in mission. Visual clarity matters. Use large fonts, readable layouts, and language that honors the intelligence of the congregation without assuming specialized knowledge. Avoid acronyms, insider terms, or unexplained shifts. If someone walks away feeling confused, they won't feel inspired.

But presentation is not only about formatting — it is about *voice*. Who presents the budget matters. Choose someone who can speak not only to the data, but to the deeper "why." Someone who carries the church's heart, not just its numbers. This may be the treasurer, pastor, moderator, or a trusted lay leader. What matters is that the presenter believes in the story being told.

Delivery should be rooted in gratitude and invitation. Thank the congregation for their faithfulness. Celebrate what God has done through their generosity. Then, gently point toward what is needed next. Avoid scarcity language. Speak instead from a place of vision and hope: "Here's what your giving has made possible — and here's what we believe God is calling us to do next."

This approach cultivates trust. And trust fosters participation.

A narrative-driven budget presentation does not require flashy media — it requires heart. It begins with a simple shift: stop talking *to* the brain, and start speaking *from* the heart. The most memorable presentations often include a short reflection from a ministry leader, a personal story from a congregant, or a few photos that remind the church of God's presence in their shared life.

Consider this: instead of beginning the presentation with "This year's operating budget totals $342,000," what if it began with, "Because of your generosity last year, 128 meals were delivered to neighbors in need, 14 children attended camp, and a lonely elder found a new church home." The number is still important — but it is placed in service of the story. People give to meaning, not math.

Some governing bodies find it helpful to organize the budget into **mission-aligned categories**, such as:

- Worship and Spiritual Formation
- Community Engagement

- Nurture and Care
- Justice and Outreach
- Infrastructure for Ministry

When the categories match the heartbeat of the church, people can see the connection more clearly. They stop seeing "staff salaries" as a cost, and begin seeing them as part of the church's investment in leadership, pastoral care, and continuity. They stop seeing "facility expenses" as a burden, and begin seeing the building as sacred ground — a place where ministry unfolds.

Of course, the spiritual tone of the presentation matters as much as the content. The way a budget is introduced sets the emotional temperature in the room. A presentation marked by nervousness or apologetic language communicates that the church should feel anxious or burdened. But a presentation rooted in gratitude, clarity, and mission-centered confidence gives people a sense of trust, excitement, and belonging.

This is especially important when the financial picture includes difficult truths. If giving is down, or cuts are needed, the governing body must be honest — but not fearful. Acknowledge the reality plainly, and then speak to the faith that sustains the church beyond numbers. Say aloud what people may be feeling: concern, fatigue, even skepticism. But then gently invite them back into the story. Remind them that the church is not held together by its budget — it is held together by God.

The best presentations include both realism and resurrection. Don't avoid the hard news. But don't stop there. Always return to the "why." Why does this matter? Why are we still here? Why are we still called?

Even something as simple as tone of voice can shift the energy in the room. Speak slowly. Pause after meaningful moments. Allow space for the weight of the mission to settle. This is not a performance — it is pastoral care. The goal is not to impress, but to invite.

When done well, a budget presentation becomes a spiritual moment. It reconnects the congregation to one another. It reminds people why they give, and what their giving makes possible. It transforms the budget from a list into a letter — written not with ink, but with Spirit.

When a church's financial plan is presented with spiritual integrity, something shifts in the room. People stop thinking, *"How much are they asking for?"* and begin wondering, *"What are we being called to do together?"* That shift is sacred. It moves the church from transaction to transformation.

This shift happens most powerfully when the congregation sees themselves reflected in the presentation. Not as passive recipients, but as active participants. Their generosity, their prayers, their effort — all of it woven into the story being told. This is especially important in congregations that have experienced financial fatigue or conflict. People need to know they are not being used for their wallets. They need to feel seen, valued, and trusted.

That's why the governing body must approach this moment with deep pastoral sensitivity. Invite feedback. Allow for questions. Be open to discomfort. When a budget is presented as a spiritual conversation rather than a financial decree, people are more likely to engage with curiosity and commitment.

It can also be helpful to connect the current budget to a longer arc. What is the church building toward over the next three years? What has changed since the last major decision point? What ministries were launched — or completed? What is emerging? Budget presentations should not be one-year snapshots. They should be chapters in a story that God is writing over time.

And while not every detail needs to be shared in a public forum, transparency builds trust. Churches must avoid the temptation to oversimplify or obscure. It is appropriate to protect individual confidentiality — such as specific staff salaries — but not to mask deficits, transfers, or financial stress. Even bad news, when shared honestly, is better received than silence. The integrity of the presentation is part of the spiritual witness of the church.

Some churches choose to present the budget in layers — beginning with the mission story, followed by a broad overview, and finally offering detailed handouts or forums for those who want to dive deeper. This approach respects different learning styles and levels of engagement. It also ensures that the governing body is not simply delivering information, but cultivating understanding.

When using visuals, choose them carefully. Avoid cluttered spreadsheets on a projector screen. Instead, use clear charts, ministry-based categories, photos of actual congregational life, and narrative captions that remind people what the numbers represent. A pie chart showing 30% of funds allocated to "Worship and Music" means far more when accompanied by a photograph of children singing on Christmas Eve or a quote from a member whose life was changed by a hymn.

And if you don't have a designer or media team? Don't worry. Heart always outweighs polish. Even a black-and-white handout becomes sacred if it connects the community to its call. The Spirit is not limited by your printer settings.

Don't underestimate the power of story. A five-minute testimony from someone impacted by the church's ministry can do more to stir generosity than an hour of charts. A photo of last summer's outreach event may say more than a spreadsheet ever could. Even a short video compilation of worship, mission, and community moments can shift the tone from obligation to celebration.

Remember: this is not just about raising money. This is about raising hope.

At its core, the church budget is not just a financial plan — it is a spiritual map. It points to where we've been, where we are, and where we believe God is leading us next. And when presented faithfully, that map becomes an invitation.

This is the sacred opportunity before every governing body: to frame the annual budget not as a request, but as a response. A response to grace. A response to Calling. A response to what the Spirit has already begun among us.

Budgets written with love, shaped in prayer, and presented with integrity will always speak louder than spreadsheets alone. They become letters of Christ — known and read by all, written not with ink, but with the Spirit of the living God.

And when that happens, people don't just give. They believe. They belong. They remember who they are and why it matters.

🕊 Discernment Questions

- Does our budget reflect what we believe God is doing in this season?
- Are we prioritizing maintenance or mission?
- How do we tell the story of ministry through our financial reports?
- What would it look like to present our budget as an act of worship?
- Where do we need to shift resources to reflect our present Calling?

Chapter 19
Compel People to Come In

Presenting the church's story and financial needs in ways that inspire generous response

"Then the master said to the servant, "Go out into the roads and lanes, and compel people to come in, so that my house may be filled."
— Luke 14:23

Jesus did not issue invitations timidly. He told stories that stirred the soul. He painted visions of what could be. He called people by name. And in the parable of the great banquet, he makes it clear: the doors of the Kingdom are flung wide, and we are to compel people to come in — not by force, but by the irresistible power of grace, welcome, and purpose.

For today's church, this call echoes through every sermon, every act of hospitality, and yes — every conversation about money. To "compel" in the spirit of Christ is not to coerce, but to *inspire*. It is to speak with such clarity of mission, such conviction of purpose, such honesty of need, and such joy in partnership that people want to be part of what God is doing.

The governing body holds a vital role in shaping how the church tells its story — and how it shares its needs. These are not separate tasks. The budget is not just an internal document. It is part of the church's public witness. The invitation to give is not just for members — it is for everyone who feels drawn into the work of love, justice, healing, and hope.

A faithful church does not manipulate, guilt, or pressure people into giving. But neither does it apologize for needing resources. When the mission is clear, the story is strong, and the invitation is sincere, people respond with generosity — not because they were convinced, but because they were *compelled*.

To compel in the way of Christ means telling the truth — about who we are, what we do, and why it matters. It means telling our story in ways that connect deeply with the longings of the human heart.

Too often, churches present their financial needs as burdens: "We're behind." "We can't keep doing this without more money." "We need to cover the gap." While these may be honest statements, they are not compelling. They speak to anxiety, not calling. They ask for pity, not partnership.

But when we reframe our needs as part of our mission — when we say, "Here is what God is doing among us, and here is what we need to keep going" — we invite people into something greater than obligation. We invite them into belonging.

Effective communication of the church's story and financial needs requires four key elements:

1. **A Clear Calling**
   People cannot support what they do not understand. Be clear. Be specific. Why does your church exist? What does it uniquely offer your community? What would be missing if your church disappeared tomorrow?
2. **A Strong Voice**
   Tone matters. Speak with conviction, not desperation. Share the need with honesty, but let the emphasis fall on vision. People are drawn to energy, not exhaustion.
3. **A Hopeful Invitation**
   Use language that includes rather than excludes. Replace "we need your money" with "we are inviting your partnership." Replace "covering expenses" with "fueling ministry."
4. **A Grateful Spirit**
   Every ask should be framed in gratitude. Not just for past giving, but for the Spirit that continues to move through the congregation. Gratitude opens hearts. Entitlement closes them.

A faithful church does not fundraise — it invites others to join in its Calling. This requires intentional storytelling. The church must be able to articulate *what God is asking of us now*, and how people's generosity can help bring that Calling to life.

When presenting financial needs, lead with the Calling. Instead of beginning with numbers, begin with vision: "We believe God is calling us to expand our food ministry so that no family in our neighborhood goes hungry." "We believe God is calling us to invest in youth, so that a new generation can grow in faith." These are not financial goals. They are spiritual commitments.

Then, and only then, explain what resources are needed to support that Calling. Be transparent about costs, but always anchor them in purpose. People are far more willing to give when they understand what their giving *does* — how it moves the church forward in God's purpose.

Churches often underestimate the power of naming their need plainly. If you need $40,000 to continue a ministry that is bearing fruit, say so. If you need new monthly givers, say how many. People are not offended by clarity — they are encouraged by it. Vague appeals create confusion. Clear invitations create commitment.

Compelling communication also means choosing the right channels and the right moments. The Sunday morning offering announcement is not the only place to tell the church's story. Use newsletters, emails, website updates, videos, testimonies, seasonal letters, and small group gatherings. Vary the format — but keep the message consistent: *This is who we are. This is what God is doing among us. This is how you can be part of it.*

When the message is grounded in Calling, the ask becomes meaningful. And when that message is shared by multiple voices — not just the pastor or treasurer — it becomes a community-wide affirmation. Invite lay leaders, ministry participants, and congregants to share why they give, and what giving has meant in their lives. Authenticity speaks louder than polish.

There is also wisdom in aligning your messaging with the seasons of the church year. During Lent, connect generosity to spiritual discipline. During Advent, frame giving as a response to the gift of Christ. In the summer, remind people how consistent giving sustains year-round ministry. In the fall, root your annual appeal in a spirit of thanksgiving and Calling into the year ahead. Every season offers a lens for the story — and an opening for generosity.

And don't neglect the practical tools. Make giving easy. Provide multiple ways to contribute — online, in person, recurring options, text-to-give. But always pair the tools with the *why*. No one is inspired by a QR code alone. They are inspired by what their giving makes possible.

Sometimes the most powerful way to compel people is to paint a picture of what could be. The governing body should not only share what resources are needed to sustain current ministry — but also name what becomes possible when the church responds boldly to God's Call.

This might sound like:
"If we meet our giving goal this year, we will be able to launch a midweek program for families who can't attend on Sundays."
"If ten new households begin giving regularly, we can expand our music ministry and include a children's choir."
"If we receive an additional $25,000 by summer, we can hire a part-time outreach coordinator to strengthen our community partnerships."

These aren't just numbers — they're possibilities. And possibility compels.

But it's not only future dreams that stir the heart. Sometimes what compels most deeply is remembering what generosity has already made possible. Take time to celebrate what God has done through the giving of this congregation. Remind them that their generosity is not theoretical — it has already borne fruit.

Share stories:

- A new member who came because of a community meal
- A child who found belonging through Sunday school
- A shut-in who receives pastoral care each week

- A teen who discovered their voice through music ministry

These are not side notes. They *are* the report. They *are* the reason we ask, the reason we give, and the reason we keep showing up to serve.

To compel is also to remind. In a world where people are constantly asked for something — time, attention, money — the church offers something else: **meaning**. Generosity in the life of the church is not another transaction. It is participation in holy work. It is alignment with God's Calling. It is an act of worship.

That is why the tone of every appeal matters. We do not beg. We bless. We do not pressure. We proclaim. We do not sell. We serve. This is not marketing. It is ministry.

And so we return, always, to the heart: God's heart for the world, our church's heart for our community, and each member's heart for something greater than themselves. When the governing body speaks from this place, people are drawn in — not because they were persuaded, but because they were *moved*.

They come to the banquet not out of guilt, but because they have glimpsed joy. They give not out of duty, but because they believe. They say yes — not because we asked well, but because God is doing something in their spirit, and they want to be part of it.

This is what it means to compel them to come in. Not with force, but with fire. Not with demand, but with devotion. Not with clever words, but with Spirit-breathed invitation.

❦ Discernment Questions

- How does our communication of financial needs reflect our Calling?
- Are we inviting people into something compelling — or just trying to cover the gap?
- What new possibilities might we name that would stir the hearts of our congregation?
- Are we using language that inspires belonging, or that reinforces obligation?
- What stories are we not telling that could help people feel more connected to our Calling?
- Have we created space for multiple voices to share why giving matters?
- How might we shift our tone from anxiety to abundance, from pressure to invitation?

Chapter 20
Bringing in the Harvest

The governing body's role in nurturing church growth, not for numbers, but for fruitfulness

So let us not grow weary in doing what is right, for we will reap at harvest time, if we do not give up... Then he said to his disciples, "The harvest is plentiful, but the laborers are few; therefore ask the Lord of the harvest to send out laborers into his harvest."
-Galatians 6:9; Matthew 9:37–38

Church growth is often discussed with anxiety. Boards ask: How do we get more people? How do we attract young families? How do we keep the doors open? But scripture gives us a different orientation. Growth is not something we manufacture. It is something we prepare for. It is something we bless when it comes. It is something we receive—not with control, but with readiness.

In Galatians, Paul reminds us that the harvest comes in season—*if we do not give up*. Jesus, in Matthew's gospel, speaks not of how to create a harvest, but how to pray for laborers to meet it. Both speak to a truth boards often forget: Our role is not to force fruit. Our role is to cultivate conditions where fruitfulness can flourish. That is the work of governance. To build structures of welcome. To focus resources on what matters. To set boundaries that keep purpose clear. To define the path and stay faithful to it, even when the fields look empty.

In church governance, growth is not the goal—it's a consequence of faithfulness. And yet, when it begins to appear—when visitors return, when ministries take root, when new leaders emerge—boards often don't know how to respond. Some celebrate too soon, assuming that numbers equal sustainability. Others grow cautious, retreating into control. Still others begin to panic, feeling unprepared to support what's unfolding.

But wise governance does not chase growth. It tends the field with care. It ensures the soil is healthy—meaning the mission is clear, the systems are sound, and the people are supported. And when the first signs of fruit appear, it doesn't rush to claim the results. It pauses, gives thanks, and strengthens the supports that helped bring it forth.

The Spirit's work cannot be forced. But it can be hindered by confusion, scarcity thinking, and misaligned leadership. It can be slowed when ministries compete for attention, when structures are too brittle to hold new energy, or when boards resist change in the name of control. Governance, in seasons of growth, must become both gardener and gatekeeper. Not the one who makes things grow—but the one who watches, discerns, and clears space for the flourishing to continue.

Sometimes the board's most faithful response to growth is restraint. Not every opportunity needs to be seized. Not every new idea requires immediate action. Growth brings with it excitement, but also urgency—and that urgency can distract from Calling. A wise board asks: Does this align with our purpose? Do we have the systems to support it? Is this a harvest we're meant to gather—or one we're meant to bless from a distance?

One board, after experiencing a surge in attendance following a community outreach event, rushed to launch multiple new ministries at once—without revisiting their Calling or evaluating their readiness. Within six months, energy had waned, leadership had thinned, and the very people they'd hoped to welcome felt abandoned. The growth was real—but the supports weren't strong enough to hold it.

Another church, by contrast, paused before expanding. They asked: What is God revealing through this increase? Where is fruit appearing—and how can we tend it slowly? They added a second worship time only after ensuring they had pastoral care systems in place. They launched small groups after training new facilitators. They did less—but with clarity. And their growth endured.

Boards often ask, "How do we measure fruitfulness?" The answer isn't simple. Numbers can tell part of the story—but not all of it. True fruitfulness is measured in alignment, transformation, and sustained participation in the church's mission. It shows up when new people feel seen and valued. When long-time members grow deeper in faith. When generosity flows naturally because people trust the direction. When ministries aren't just busy—but life-giving.

The board's job is not to tally the yield, but to discern the signs of health. Not to push the process, but to protect it. Growth is not a trophy—it's a trust. And when it comes, it's not a moment to boast, but a moment to bless. The results are not ours to own. They are the Spirit's to reveal. Our role is to be found faithful in the tending.

This is why spiritual discernment must be part of every board conversation about growth. Without it, churches chase trends instead of truths. They replicate what worked elsewhere without asking what fits here. But with it, even small growth is honored rightly. Even quiet fruit is celebrated with humility. And even a pause in growth is not seen as failure—but as time to deepen roots.

Preparing for Growth Before It Comes

One of the board's most sacred roles is to prepare the church to receive what it prays for. Too often, we ask God for growth without making space for it. We plant and water but forget to build the storehouse. We create entry points for new people but forget to create support structures once they arrive. True readiness is not reactive. It's proactive. It's what governance does behind the scenes so that ministry can flourish in the open.

This preparation includes tangible actions: building a strong onboarding process for new leaders, clarifying ministry responsibilities, ensuring that communication systems are welcoming and consistent, reviewing space usage and facility access. But it also includes spiritual alignment: Are we asking for growth out of anxiety or Calling? Do we trust the Spirit to bring the increase in God's time—or are we demanding fruit on our schedule?

A church may not be numerically growing today, but a faithful board will still ask: If the harvest came tomorrow, would we be ready? Would our policies support it? Would our people sustain it? Would our leadership structure encourage it or collapse under it? These are not questions of doubt. They are questions of faith. Faith that God desires to bring new life—and wisdom enough to prepare for it with open hands and clear hearts.

The Tension Between Mission and Capacity

There's a moment every healthy board must face: when the church's mission reaches beyond its current capacity. It's not a failure. It's a sign that growth is happening—or is about to. But if left unexamined, it can fracture the very systems that were once strong. When momentum builds faster than infrastructure, ministry leaders burn out. When vision expands without staffing or budget support, people begin to feel used instead of valued.

One transcript story described a board that launched a new worship service, expanded children's ministry, and added a community food pantry—all within the same six months. Each effort was rooted in mission. But they underestimated the toll on their volunteers. Within a year, two key leaders had stepped down, several ministries were consolidated out of exhaustion, and trust was damaged—not because the ideas were wrong, but because the board failed to pace the implementation.

This is where the board's discernment is critical. Every opportunity must be weighed not only by its alignment with mission, but by its timing and support. The question isn't just "Is this a good idea?" but "Can we sustain this faithfully right now?" If not, it may be an idea to bless for the future—or one to pursue in partnership with others.

Discerning with Courage, Not Control

Church boards often confuse discernment with hesitation. They fear that slowing down will be seen as resistance to growth. But spiritual governance isn't about holding back—it's about listening deeply before moving forward. Discernment asks: Are we moving with the Spirit, or just responding to pressure? Is our pace prayerful, or reactive? Are we saying yes because we are called—or because we are afraid to disappoint?

Courageous boards do not say yes to everything. They say yes to what aligns with Calling. They say no to what stretches the church beyond health. And they say "not yet" when they sense the need to strengthen the foundation before building the next level.

From the transcript, one board leader shared: "We kept saying yes because it was good work. But good doesn't always mean faithful. And we eventually realized—we were working harder, not listening better." That insight led them to pause several new initiatives, spend a season in prayer and planning, and later relaunch with greater clarity and support. What had once felt like retreat became the soil for sustainable renewal.

Governance rooted in the Spirit does not fear evaluation. It trusts that even in times of pruning, fruitfulness is being prepared. That's the heart of discernment in times of growth—not to deny the harvest, but to tend it with wisdom.

🕊 Discernment Questions

- What signs of spiritual growth are we seeing—and how are we supporting them?
- Are we building the systems needed to sustain what God is growing?
- Where might we be rushing ahead instead of discerning the season?
- Have we confused visible momentum with faithful readiness?
- What is God asking us to tend—not just measure?

Chapter 21
Leaving an Inheritance

Planning for the future through endowments, reserves, and long-term financial vision

"The good leave an inheritance to their children's children…"
– Proverbs 13:22

Faithful ministry requires long vision. While the day-to-day decisions of a governing body often focus on immediate needs, true stewardship means planning for a future we may never see. We plant trees whose shade we may not enjoy. We build reserves not out of fear, but out of trust — trust that God will continue to call, continue to send, and continue to work through those who follow.

In the wisdom literature of scripture, an inheritance is more than wealth — it is a legacy. It is the passing down of purpose, of wisdom, of possibility. The governing body is entrusted not only with today's resources, but with the foresight to preserve, protect, and position the church to live its Calling for generations to come.

This chapter explores how churches can develop and manage endowments, reserves, and restricted funds in ways that are spiritually aligned, legally sound, and practically sustainable. When handled well, these tools do not constrain the church — they *liberate* it, ensuring that its faithfulness can continue even through disruption, transition, or decline.

Planned giving is one of the most underutilized opportunities in congregational life — not because people are unwilling to give, but because churches rarely talk about it with clarity, comfort, or confidence. Yet among the most faithful in our pews are those who would gladly leave a legacy, if only they were invited to do so.

As spiritual leaders, governing bodies must learn to help people **continue to give beyond their time on this earth**. This is not about asking for money in moments of grief — it is about cultivating a long-term vision of generosity that begins with gratitude, grows through trust, and culminates in legacy.

Planned giving allows individuals and families to shape the future of ministry in ways that reflect their values and Calling. Whether through bequests, beneficiary designations, charitable trusts, or gifts of property, these commitments become a kind of spiritual testament — a final act of witness that says: *"This mattered to me. I believe it should continue."*

To encourage this, churches must first create space for the conversation. This means naming legacy giving in newsletters and annual reports, offering workshops or Q&A sessions, and partnering with estate professionals who can answer questions in faithful, practical ways. It also means honoring those who have already included the church in their plans — not with flashy plaques, but with genuine thanks.

When someone chooses to leave a gift to the church in their will, they are not merely being generous. They are entrusting the church with a piece of their story. The governing body's role is to receive that story with reverence, and to steward it with care.

An endowment is one of the most powerful tools a church can use to carry its Calling into the future. But only when it is understood — and governed — with wisdom. Too often, churches either avoid creating endowments altogether or mismanage them through vague intentions, poor oversight, or a false belief that "we're too small to need one."

The truth is this: endowments, when properly established, can stabilize ministry, protect against economic uncertainty, and ensure that core commitments remain funded even in lean years. More than that, they offer members a way to *continue giving beyond their time on this earth* — and to do so in a way that aligns with their deepest values.

The Managing Endowments webinar and PowerPoint identify three primary fund types that every board must understand:

1. **Undesignated Funds**
   These are unrestricted gifts, including regular tithes and offerings, general contributions, and grants not tied to specific outcomes. They are essential to daily operations but should not be confused with legacy gifts, which often carry a deeper sense of purpose.
2. **Designated Funds**
   Set aside by the governing body for a specific internal

purpose — such as building maintenance or capital improvement — these funds can be released or redirected if priorities shift. Their flexibility is a gift, but they require clear documentation and communication.

3. **Restricted Funds**
Given by donors for a specific purpose, these carry legal and ethical obligations. Restrictions can be temporary (e.g., for this year's youth trip) or permanent (e.g., a named scholarship fund). These funds belong not to the church, but to the intention of the donor, and must be managed with careful accounting and spiritual integrity.

Managing restricted and endowed funds requires both spiritual and legal attentiveness. Once a church accepts a gift with restrictions — especially for long-term or permanent use — it also accepts the responsibility to **honor that gift in perpetuity**, or until a legal and ethical release is obtained.

This is where governing bodies must become familiar with the **Uniform Prudent Management of Institutional Funds Act (UPMIFA)**, which offers a framework for investment and spending that balances present needs with future sustainability. UPMIFA encourages a *total return approach* — allowing churches to consider both income (like dividends) and asset appreciation when determining an annual draw. This ensures that the fund remains resilient, especially during market fluctuations.

Most experts recommend a **prudent draw rate** — typically around 4–5% annually — though this can be adjusted depending on economic conditions and the fund's purpose. The goal is to preserve the fund's long-term value while allowing for consistent, responsible use.

The governing body must also ensure that restricted funds are:

- **Segregated in accounting** — never co-mingled with general operating funds

- **Tracked separately** — with clear documentation of income, use, and remaining balances
- **Reported regularly** — both to internal stakeholders and, when appropriate, to donors or their representatives

Transparency is not just good practice — it is a form of reverence. These gifts were given with trust. Our stewardship of them must reflect that trust.

Occasionally, a church may need to release or revise a restriction. In the case of designated funds (set by the board), this can usually be done through a formal board action. But for donor-restricted funds, **only the original donor** — or, in some cases, the state attorney general or a court — has the authority to release the restriction. Churches must never assume they can simply "repurpose" such gifts. Legal counsel should always be consulted in these cases.

To sustain long-term generosity and protect the integrity of the church, the governing body must also establish clear **policies** related to planned giving, endowments, and restricted funds. These include:

- **Gift Acceptance Policy** — clarifying what types of gifts the church will and will not accept (e.g., property, stocks, restricted donations, naming rights)
- **Investment Policy** — outlining the church's approach to risk, diversification, ethical investing, and draw rates
- **Fundraising Policy** — ensuring that public appeals are aligned with the church's Calling and don't unintentionally create permanent restrictions

These documents are not bureaucratic burdens — they are **spiritual boundary markers**. They protect the church from acting out of desperation or confusion, and they provide clarity when future leaders are no longer familiar with the original circumstances of a gift.

Churches must also educate their leaders and staff. Board members, pastors, and treasurers should all be familiar with how to talk about legacy giving in ways that are invitational and respectful. No one wants to feel pressured — but many would welcome the opportunity to leave a lasting impact if given the tools and the trust.

Communication is essential. Invite conversation. Share stories of previous legacy gifts and the ministry they've made possible. Consider creating a **Legacy Circle** — a simple way of honoring those who have included the church in their plans. Public recognition is not about ego; it's about testimony. When one person gives in this way, it gives others permission to consider the same.

Ultimately, endowments and reserves are not about accumulating wealth. They are about sustaining faithfulness. They are not about hoarding for fear of scarcity. They are about positioning the church to say yes to its Calling, even in uncertain times.

There is a deep and holy wisdom in preparing for the needs of a church we may never personally see. When we help people continue to give beyond their time on this earth, we create a legacy of trust — trust that the Spirit will still be speaking, that the church will still be listening, and that the ministries we've nurtured will still be bearing fruit.

This long-view stewardship does more than secure financial resources. It strengthens spiritual imagination. It invites every generation to see themselves not only as recipients of the church's past, but as co-creators of its future.

It is easy to focus on the urgent: this year's budget, this month's shortfall, today's broken boiler. But the governing body must also hold space for the eternal: the slow, steady faithfulness of those who plant seeds without expecting to see the harvest. These are the saints who built the sanctuary, established the scholarship fund, or left a bequest that now funds a ministry none of them lived to witness.

We honor them not by preserving the past, but by ensuring that their generosity continues to breathe life into the church's future.

Churches that embrace planned giving and long-term financial planning often find that it reshapes their entire posture. Scarcity gives way to stability. Panic gives way to purpose. Short-term thinking gives way to generational vision.

And when the time comes to draw from these funds — in a crisis, in a moment of opportunity, or in the simple rhythm of yearly ministry — it is not done with anxiety. It is done with gratitude.

Discernment Questions

- What legacy are we preparing—financially and spiritually?
- Do our endowment or reserve policies reflect long-term Calling or short-term caution?
- How do we ensure that today's decisions bless future leaders?
- Are we communicating clearly about the purpose and limits of restricted gifts?
- What seeds can we plant now that will support ministry beyond our own leadership?

Chapter 22
Threads to Refuse

Knowing when to say no, and how to protect the integrity of our Calling

I have sworn to the Lord, God Most High, creator of heaven and earth, that I will not take a thread or a sandal strap or anything that is yours, so that you might not say, "I made Abram rich."
-Genesis 14:22–23

Not every gift is a blessing. Not every opportunity is meant for us. Not every offer is aligned with our Calling. And saying "no" can be one of the most faithful things a board ever does.

When Abram refused the spoils of war from the king of Sodom, it wasn't about pride. It was about purpose. He knew what was at stake: the clarity of who he served and what defined his legacy. He refused the thread, the sandal strap, and the credit. Not out of fear—but out of reverence. He knew that accepting the wrong thing could cloud the witness of the right one.

Church boards often assume their job is to say yes to what is helpful. But part of spiritual leadership is learning to say no—even when the gift is generous, the project exciting, or the opportunity timely. Because sometimes, beneath the surface of a good offer is a thread that pulls the church off course. And it only takes a thread to unravel the whole.

Church boards are called to protect not just assets, but alignment. And that means developing the discernment to notice when a good thing could become a costly distraction. Sometimes the cost is spiritual—accepting a gift that requires the church to shift its values. Sometimes it's relational—agreeing to something that ties leadership to an individual's expectations. Sometimes it's organizational—a program or campaign that, though well-funded, fractures the focus of the church.

This is why saying no isn't just about risk avoidance. It's about protecting clarity. And clarity is the foundation of mission. In the transcripts from the *Managing Endowments* webinar, a board member described a large gift that was offered to fund a "legacy building" for youth ministry. But it came with a stipulation: the church had to rename part of the campus and restructure existing programs. It took months to evaluate—and ultimately, they said no. Not because they lacked appreciation, but because the strings would have shifted the church's direction. The gift was generous. But it wasn't aligned.

To refuse the wrong threads, churches must first know what fabric they're weaving. When a congregation is unclear about its purpose, everything looks like an opportunity. But when the Calling is clear, decisions become simpler. The right gifts affirm the mission. The wrong ones—however appealing—reveal themselves through prayer and process.

Boards must develop the courage to say: "Thank you, but no." Not harshly. Not fearfully. But with peace and conviction. Because the integrity of the church is not just protected through accounting—it is preserved through boundaries.

This doesn't mean every offer is suspect. Many gifts are Spirit-led and mission-aligned. But even good gifts need faithful filters. And that's where the board's responsibility becomes not just financial, but pastoral. To ask questions others may not think to ask. To pause where others might rush. To name the weight that comes with generosity—and to carry it with wisdom, or not at all.

These filters aren't about distrust. They're about design. Healthy churches establish systems to help them discern in advance: What types of gifts will we accept? What restrictions are appropriate—and which ones create confusion? How do we evaluate designated giving, planned gifts, real estate, naming rights, or anonymous donations? These policies must be shaped by theological identity, not just legal counsel. Because the real question isn't, "Can we accept this?" It's "Should we?"

That's why every church needs a **Gift Acceptance Policy**—not hidden in a file, but discussed at the board level. A policy that doesn't just say how, but why. One that helps a future board decline an offer with clarity, even if today's leaders are tempted by need. It should include guidelines about donor influence, long-term obligations, and how to communicate refusal without damaging relationships. The goal isn't protection from people. It's protection of purpose.

As one pastor shared during the *Managing Endowments* session: "It's not about guarding the door—it's about keeping the path clear." That's the posture of this kind of discernment. Not defensive. Not dismissive. Just deeply committed to walking in step with the Spirit, even when the world offers a shortcut.

Sometimes the pressure to accept a gift comes not from outside, but from within. A congregation facing financial stress may be tempted to accept funds with strings because "we need the money." A well-meaning board may override its policies in order to say yes to a beloved member's offer. But faithful governance resists the pull of urgency. It listens beneath the surface. It asks, "What will this cost us—not just in dollars, but in direction?"

One church received a large donation earmarked for technology upgrades—but only if the donor could choose the vendor and direct the implementation. At first, it seemed manageable. The church needed the equipment. The offer was timely. But within weeks, the donor's involvement became supervisory. Volunteers felt sidelined. Staff felt controlled. What began as a gift became a shadow structure of influence. Eventually, the board had to renegotiate the arrangement—and the fallout damaged trust on all sides.

This is why discernment must be part of the board's rhythm—not just when crises arise, but as a proactive discipline. It's why every major financial decision—especially those tied to restricted gifts, endowments, or naming—should include space for silence, scripture, shared wisdom, and slow reflection. These aren't delays. They're the sacred pauses that keep the path clear.

Discernment is not a tool to say no to everything. It's a posture that says yes only to what God is asking us to carry. And sometimes, that means protecting the Calling from the weight of someone else's expectations—even when those expectations come wrapped in generosity.

The truth is: what a church refuses can define it just as much as what it accepts. Abram didn't reject the king's offer out of pride. He did it out of clarity. He knew that his story needed to point to God, not to human favor. And the same is true today. When a church says no with peace, it is saying yes to something deeper. Yes to mission. Yes to integrity. Yes to the slow, steady work of faithfulness.

That kind of clarity builds trust over time. It lets future leaders lead without confusion. It tells the congregation: We are not for sale. Our direction is not determined by the highest bidder. We are not afraid to walk away from good things if they are not the right things. Because our provision does not come from any one person. It comes from God.

🕊 Discernment Questions

- Have we ever accepted a gift or opportunity that pulled us off course?
- What policies guide us in discerning when to say no—and are we following them?
- Are we willing to walk away from resources that compromise our values?
- What safeguards protect the integrity of our Calling, even under pressure?
- Where do we need courage to set clearer boundaries in our financial decisions?

Part Five: Leading With Grace in Difficult Times

"But he said to me, 'My grace is sufficient for you, for power is made perfect in weakness.' So, I will boast all the more gladly of my weaknesses, so that the power of Christ may dwell in me."

– 2 Corinthians 12:9

Part Five:

Leading With Grace in Difficult Times

This section reminds us that church governance is not about control—it's about care. These chapters focus on long-term sustainability, resilience, and unity. We end where we began: as a people called together by God.

- Guardians of the Flame
- When the Path Is Difficult
- Unity in Calling

Chapter 23
Blessed Are the Peacemakers

Governance's sacred
responsibility in healing division
and leading toward unity

"Blessed are the peacemakers, for they will be called children of God."
– Matthew 5:9

In every congregation, moments arise when tension flares, conflict brews, or division threatens to take root. It is tempting to believe that unity means everyone agrees, but biblical peace is not the absence of conflict—it is the presence of right relationship. The work of peace is not passive; it is proactive, prayerful, and deeply spiritual. In seasons of tension, the governing body is not called to remain neutral or avoid discomfort—it is called to lead with grace and conviction.

When Jesus declared "Blessed are the peacemakers," he did not say "peacekeepers." The difference is profound. Peacekeeping avoids conflict at all costs. Peacemaking steps into conflict with courage, trusting in God's healing power and calling forth a better way. Governance teams are uniquely positioned to lead this sacred work.

Conflict Is Not the Enemy

The presence of conflict does not mean something is wrong—it often means something important is trying to emerge. In a church where people care deeply, disagreement is inevitable. What determines whether it becomes destructive or constructive is how leadership responds. When conflict is mishandled, it can breed mistrust, splinter relationships, and paralyze ministry. When addressed with spiritual wisdom and humility, it can clarify the congregation's call and deepen bonds of trust.

As one governing board member shared, "The turning point in our conflict wasn't the day we all agreed—it was the day we all started listening again."

Rather than asking how to prevent all conflict, governing bodies should ask how they are preparing themselves to respond faithfully when it arises. This includes building systems of communication, nurturing trust, and committing to early engagement before tension becomes harm.

Common Sources of Disunity

While every church has its own story, many conflicts share familiar roots:

- **Lack of clear mission or vision** – Without a compelling and shared sense of purpose, members pursue their own interpretations of what the church should be doing. This divergence fosters frustration and fatigue.
- **Ambiguous roles and authority** – When boundaries between leadership roles are blurred or poorly defined, power struggles and accusations of overreach become more likely.
- **Broken or untrusted decision-making processes** – When congregants don't understand how decisions are made—or worse, suspect decisions are made behind closed doors—distrust builds.
- **Unspoken emotional wounds** – Old grievances and relational breakdowns, especially when left unaddressed, can poison the well of cooperation.
- **Cultural, racial, or generational divides** – A diverse church is a blessing, but without intentional dialogue and spiritual curiosity, diversity can lead to misunderstanding or exclusion.

None of these issues are purely procedural. They are **spiritual wounds**, and the governing body has a sacred responsibility to name them, tend them, and seek restoration.

The Governing Body's Role in Unity

The call of governance is not just to manage the church's affairs—it is to **steward its unity**. This means governing bodies must:

- **Set the tone** by modeling mature, respectful dialogue even when disagreement arises
- **Clarify roles and expectations**, reducing opportunities for confusion or overlap

- **Build trust in decision-making**, making the process transparent, fair, and participatory
- **Surface and name points of tension early**, before they calcify into hardened divisions
- **Create space for truth-telling**, where all voices can be heard without fear

These are not administrative tasks. They are ministries of peace.

Early Engagement: Preventing Division Before It Spreads

Peacemaking does not begin after conflict explodes—it begins long before. The governing body's commitment to early engagement is one of the most effective ways to maintain the health of the congregation. This means noticing subtle shifts in tone, listening for what is not being said, and creating regular opportunities for open conversation.

One pastor recalled a moment when a board meeting became unusually tense. "Something in the room had shifted," she said. "It wasn't what people were saying—it was what they were withholding." That moment led to a facilitated conversation that revealed a deeper concern about leadership transparency. Because the board chose to stop and listen early, the situation did not escalate.

To support early resolution, governing bodies can:

- Include **regular "check-in" spaces** during meetings for members to voice concerns
- Use **anonymous pulse surveys** to gauge emotional temperature in the congregation
- Establish a **clear path for feedback** that does not require formal complaints
- Invite an outside facilitator when discussions become emotionally charged

Building a Culture of Respectful Communication

Unity is not possible without healthy communication. Governing body members must lead by example. This means practicing not just **what** we say, but **how** we say it.

Every meeting, conversation, and communication from the board should reinforce:

- **Respect for every voice** — no interrupting, dismissiveness, or sarcasm
- **Clarity over assumptions** — ask for clarification rather than jumping to conclusions
- **Curiosity over defensiveness** — respond with "help me understand" instead of rebuttal
- **Grace over accusation** — assume the best even when misunderstandings arise

A single board member who models these values can shift the entire culture of a meeting. A full board who commits to them can shift the trajectory of a church.

The Cost of Avoidance

Churches often fall into the trap of believing that avoiding conflict is a form of peace. But avoidance is not peace—it is postponement. Left unaddressed, conflict festers. Small misunderstandings grow into hardened narratives. People retreat, disengage, or quietly exit. Ministries grind to a halt as emotional energy is consumed by what goes unspoken.

One small congregation in rural Illinois learned this the hard way. A disagreement over the use of fellowship hall space turned into a years-long rift between two prominent families. At first, leaders hoped it would "blow over." It didn't. Over time, it began to influence budget decisions, worship attendance, and even who volunteered for what. When a new moderator finally invited both families to share their stories in a structured circle led by a regional minister, the depth of pain became clear—and so did the missed opportunities for early intervention.

That congregation is healing now, but the process took years. As one leader reflected, "We were trying to protect the church by not talking about it. But silence became its own kind of damage."

For governing bodies, the takeaway is this: **The longer we wait to respond to conflict, the more expensive it becomes—emotionally, spiritually, and often financially.** Avoidance erodes trust in leadership, discourages participation, and may cause gifted people to walk away.

Systems That Prevent Division

Peacemaking is not just reactive. Wise boards build **governance systems** that help prevent conflict before it takes root.

These systems include:

- **Clear bylaws and operating procedures** that define how decisions are made and who holds which responsibilities
- **Well-communicated roles** so ministry leaders, staff, and volunteers understand their authority and limits
- **A transparent decision-making process**, where input is gathered and decisions are communicated consistently
- **Healthy meeting structures**, including open agendas, time for prayer and reflection, and regular check-ins

One urban congregation in California found that simply updating its bylaws to clarify decision-making roles eliminated most of the conflict between its board and pastoral staff. What had felt personal was actually systemic. The structure, once clarified, allowed for collaboration instead of competition.

Even small churches can take simple steps to build this clarity:

- Write down **job descriptions** for volunteer roles

- Offer **basic conflict training** at annual retreats or leadership gatherings
- Establish a **"covenant of communication"** for board members that outlines expected behaviors

These are acts of spiritual stewardship, not bureaucratic exercises. **When the structure is sound, the spirit can flow freely.**

The Ministry of Listening

At the heart of peacemaking is the practice of listening—not just to words, but to the Spirit moving through the people. Governing bodies must develop the discipline of **listening beneath the surface**: to grief disguised as anger, to fear hiding behind resistance, to longing veiled in complaint.

This kind of listening is not passive. It is an act of **spiritual hospitality**. It makes room for pain without rushing to fix it. It honors each voice without demanding agreement. It believes God may be speaking even through dissent.

In one congregation undergoing a pastoral transition, the governing board set up a series of "listening circles" with trained facilitators. Each circle invited congregants to share their hopes, concerns, and experiences of the past few years. What emerged was not just a list of complaints—it was a story of a congregation longing to be heard. The act of listening alone diffused much of the tension. People felt seen, and that became the first step toward healing.

Listening is sacred work. It slows us down. It makes space for truth. It is, perhaps, the most radical act of peacemaking a board can offer.

Trust Takes Time — and Intention

Once trust is broken—whether by mishandled conflict, secrecy, or a sense of spiritual abandonment—it must be rebuilt with care.

Governing bodies that seek to be peacemakers must understand that **restoring trust is not a moment. It is a ministry.**

Restoration requires:

- **Acknowledging the harm** – Silence deepens mistrust. Even when leadership did not cause the harm, it can acknowledge it.
- **Creating small wins** – Consistent follow-through on simple commitments demonstrates reliability.
- **Rituals of healing** – A liturgy of confession and forgiveness, a shared prayer service, or a moment of communal recommitment can open hearts again.
- **Vulnerable leadership** – Admitting mistakes models courage and signals safety. One board chair who began a meeting with, "We didn't handle this well, and I'm sorry," changed the temperature of the entire room.

This work cannot be rushed. But it must be led. In times of disunity, people look to the board not just for decisions—but for direction, tone, and spiritual courage.

Reconciliation Requires Structures

Forgiveness is a spiritual necessity, but reconciliation is a process. Healthy churches build **structures that support reconciliation** when harm occurs.

These may include:

- **A clear grievance process** – not to encourage complaints, but to make space for real concerns to be named and addressed
- **A care or reconciliation team** – trained lay leaders who can help mediate or walk alongside members in times of tension

- **Regular review of church climate** – a short annual survey or small-group feedback sessions that surface unseen conflict early

Small congregations may not have the capacity for formal teams, but even a committed **pair of trusted elders** who offer a listening ear and prayer can serve this function. What matters is that the congregation knows reconciliation is not an afterthought—it is part of the church's way of being.

One board member described reconciliation this way: "We thought our job was to solve problems. But what God was really asking us to do was hold space for grace."

Leading With Courage in the Midst of Disagreement

Not all conflict is about harm. Sometimes, faithful people simply see things differently. These moments, too, are opportunities for spiritual leadership.

Boards often fear disagreement because it feels like failure. But diversity of thought can be a sign of health—when it's rooted in love. The key is not to eliminate disagreement but to **navigate it with spiritual maturity**.

This requires:

- **Centering the conversation on God's calling**, not personal preference
- **Naming shared values**, even when proposed paths diverge
- **Making room for silence and prayer** when discussion becomes heated
- **Discerning, not debating**—using sacred listening, not just argument

A rural congregation preparing to repurpose their education wing faced deep disagreement. Some wanted to lease it for revenue;

others envisioned a center for youth. The board paused their vote and invited three weeks of prayer, small-group reflection, and scripture-based discernment before returning to the table. In that space, something shifted. New possibilities emerged that honored both visions. What had felt like a standoff became a breakthrough.

Courageous governance is not about "getting to yes"—it's about getting to God's truth together.

The Spiritual Cost of Division

When division lingers, it leaves more than strained relationships—it erodes mission. Energy is spent managing tension instead of releasing vision. Leaders grow weary, not from their calling, but from navigating conflict that was never addressed. The community begins to protect itself instead of offering itself. And slowly, what was once vibrant becomes heavy. Not broken. But burdened.

Church boards are entrusted with more than policy and finance. They are entrusted with the spiritual climate of the body. This doesn't mean resolving every conflict. It means refusing to ignore them. It means being the ones who name what others fear to say. Who hold the circle when it wants to break. Who pray not just for resolution, but for renewal.

Peacemaking is not weakness. It is not passivity. It is the courage to say: "This matters. You matter. We matter enough to try again." The board's role is to create the conditions for that trying. For listening. For apology. For lament. For healing. Not once—but as a rhythm. As a reflection of Christ's own ministry.

This is what Paul meant when he spoke of the ministry of reconciliation. Not a one-time event. A way of being. A commitment to leading with open hands and whole hearts. Not to control outcomes, but to clear the way for communion. Let the answer be grace. Let the process be sacred. Let your leadership be a living invitation to unity—imperfect, but real.

A Final Word to Leaders

You will not always get it right. You will sometimes avoid conflict too long, or respond too quickly. You will make decisions that some celebrate and others question. That is the burden and the beauty of spiritual leadership.

But take heart. Christ does not bless the perfect—he blesses the peacemakers.

May your leadership reflect the One who stepped into the world's greatest conflict and made peace not through power, but through love.

🕊 **Discernment Questions**

- What is one practice we can begin this month to build trust and transparency?
- Who in our congregation might need an invitation to speak what has been unspoken?
- How do we discern when to pause for healing and when to move forward in faith?
- Are we leading our church toward peace—or simply avoiding discomfort?
- How might we invite Christ's example of grace into our leadership today?

Chapter 24
Healed and Whole Again

Creating a path toward reconciliation, restoration, and rebuilding after harm or loss

Your ancient ruins shall be rebuilt; you shall raise up the foundations of many generations; you shall be called the repairer of the breach, the restorer of streets to live in.
-Isaiah 58:12

In the life of every congregation, there are moments that leave a mark. A painful leadership transition. A moral failure. An unresolved conflict. A slow season of loss that no one talks about aloud. The grief lingers, even as the bulletins get printed and the meetings resume. Ministry continues, but the soul of the church feels quieter, heavier.

This is the sacred moment when governance becomes a ministry of healing.

Healing is not the same as recovery. Recovery may bring the numbers back. Healing brings the people back to each other. It rebuilds trust. It restores hope. It allows a congregation to say, "This happened—and by God's grace, we are still here."

The governing body cannot rush this process, but it can shape it. It can hold space for grief. It can model truth-telling. It can name the harm without shame. And it can walk with the congregation toward a future that is honest, whole, and aligned again with God's calling.

This is not administrative work. It is spiritual work. And it is holy.

Recognizing the Wounds

Before healing can begin, leaders must first recognize that harm has occurred. In some churches, the pain is obvious—a public conflict, a pastoral misconduct, a church split. In others, the wounds are quiet and unspoken, carried in the tone of conversations, in who no longer shows up, or in the energy that once fueled ministry but now feels absent.

Boards that lead with wisdom know to look beneath the surface. What seems like resistance to new ideas may be a symptom of fear. What looks like apathy may in fact be unresolved grief. What sounds like anger may be unspoken disappointment.

One congregation on the East Coast experienced a painful pastoral transition marked by accusations, defensive silence, and broken relationships. The new governing board, appointed after the resignation, quickly realized they could not begin moving forward without first addressing what had been left unspoken. Instead of launching new initiatives, they held a series of healing gatherings—story circles, shared prayer, and small group conversations focused on truth-telling. Only after that season of reflection did they begin the process of strategic planning. Their timeline was slower. But their foundation was stronger.

Governance teams must ask: Are we trying to lead people forward before they have had space to heal?

Restoration Is Not Repair

It's tempting to believe that healing is about putting things back the way they were. But restoration is not the same as repair. Restoration doesn't erase the past—it integrates it. It asks what must be honored, what must be grieved, and what must be surrendered.

Biblical restoration always leads to transformation. The wall Nehemiah rebuilt wasn't the same as before. The people returning from exile didn't recreate the old temple—they discovered new rhythms of faithfulness. Churches too must learn how to tell the truth about what was lost, while embracing what is still possible.

This means:

- Allowing **space for lament**—without rushing to resolution
- Holding **rituals of remembrance** or acknowledgment
- Telling the truth in public, not just behind closed doors
- Listening to those who were most affected—even if it is uncomfortable

One church board in the Midwest scheduled a special worship service on the one-year anniversary of a painful split. The service was not about blame. It was about honoring the grief, acknowledging the loss, and recommitting to one another. That service, more than any program, marked the beginning of healing.

Governing bodies set the tone. Will the church rush to move on—or will it move forward, whole and honest?

Rebuilding Trust Through Consistency and Care

Trust, once broken, cannot be restored by declarations. It is rebuilt slowly, through consistent action and visible integrity. The governing body plays a central role in creating the conditions where trust can grow again—not by demanding it, but by earning it.

This means:

- **Communicating transparently**, even when the news is hard
- **Following through on commitments**, no matter how small
- **Owning past mistakes**, even if leadership has changed
- **Inviting feedback**, not just offering information

Congregations notice what leaders do, not just what they say. A board that meets regularly, posts its minutes, responds to concerns with kindness, and returns phone calls is quietly building trust. These mundane acts are sacred when done in a spirit of restoration.

For small or volunteer-led churches, the practices need not be complex. A printed board update in the weekly bulletin. A quarterly listening session. A board member who checks in personally with those who've pulled away. The point is not perfection—the point is presence.

In one small church recovering from a history of secrecy and top-down decision-making, the moderator began each board meeting by reading aloud the board's covenant: "We speak the truth in love. We honor every voice. We do not hide from hard things." Over time, the congregation noticed. People began to re-engage. Trust was not declared—it was demonstrated.

The Role of Ritual and Sacred Action

Words alone are not enough. In the life of the church, healing requires **ritual**—embodied, communal acts that invite the Spirit to mend what human effort cannot.

These might include:

- A service of **lament and hope**, inviting members to bring forward written prayers or memories
- A **recommitment ritual**, where leaders or the congregation speak aloud their hopes for the future
- A visual **"healing wall"** where congregants write messages of reconciliation or remembrance
- A simple act of **laying hands** and praying over a newly formed leadership team

In churches where trust has been broken, especially by those in leadership, such rituals should be offered with humility, not fanfare. They are not announcements of closure—they are invitations to continue the work together, under the guidance of the Spirit.

Congregational restoration is not something the board "leads" from above. It is something the board **participates in**, modeling honesty, patience, and grace.

Restoring Relationships Within the Body

No congregation can be whole when its members are estranged. In the aftermath of conflict or loss, restoring relationships becomes a central task of faithful governance. This is not simply about encouraging people to "forgive and forget"—it is about **creating the conditions for reconciliation** to unfold.

This process includes:

- **Identifying broken relationships** within the church body and inviting dialogue
- **Equipping lay leaders** with basic skills in listening, de-escalation, and mediation
- **Offering structured opportunities** for reconnection, such as healing circles, shared meals, or facilitated conversations
- **Ensuring that everyone knows** where they can turn when relationships feel strained

Some congregations designate a small team of spiritually mature members—often deacons, elders, or retired leaders—to serve as a "Care and Reconciliation Team." Their work is quiet and pastoral. They listen to grievances, offer spiritual support, and, when needed, help individuals take the first step toward reconciliation. In smaller congregations, this function can be carried out by the board itself or a trusted elder who serves as a confidential sounding board.

But reconciliation is not always about resolution. Sometimes, the most faithful outcome is not agreement but renewed respect. The goal is not uniformity. It is community—rooted in God's love, not personal victory.

A pastor once reflected, "We thought peacemaking meant everyone hugging at the end. What it really meant was giving each other space to be honest, and still choosing to stay at the table."

Boards that encourage truth and humility over "quick fixes" foster spiritual maturity in the congregation. And that maturity becomes the soil in which new growth is possible.

Returning to the Call

The final stage of healing is not just about being at peace—it is about **reconnecting with purpose**. Many congregations, once harmed, lose their sense of direction. They become reactive, cautious, or overly inward. The governing body's sacred responsibility is to gently and consistently reorient the church toward its **God-given calling**.

This does not mean launching a flurry of new programs. It means asking simple, grounding questions:

- What have we learned about ourselves?
- What does God still want to do through us?
- How can we move forward with honesty and hope?

Some boards engage in a brief season of discernment, inviting the congregation into reflection and prayer around what God is calling them to next. Others return to a previously articulated vision with fresh perspective. In either case, the governing body becomes a guide—not pushing, but **reminding the church that healing is not the end of the journey—it is the beginning of a new one.**

A healed church is not a church without scars. It is a church that bears witness to the God who rebuilds ruins and makes the broken whole.

Discernment Questions

- What wounds from our church's past may still need to be named aloud?
- Where might we be trying to "move on" rather than "move through" a season of loss?
- How can we rebuild trust in ways that are simple, visible, and rooted in grace?
- What rituals or communal acts might help us honor the past and re-commit to our future?
- Are we helping our congregation return to its call—or simply return to routine?

Chapter 25
Iron Sharpens Iron

Navigating disagreement, conflict, and decision-making with courage and care

Iron sharpens iron, and one person sharpens the wits of another.
-Proverbs 27:17

Speaking the truth in love, we must grow up in every way into him who is the head, into Christ.
-Ephesians 4:15

In a community centered on love, disagreement may seem like something to avoid. But the Church is not called to uniformity—it is called to unity. Disagreement, when engaged with spiritual maturity, becomes a source of growth. Conflict, when rooted in mutual respect, becomes a crucible for discernment. The governing body must be equipped not to eliminate tension, but to **steward it wisely**.

The work of governance does not require everyone to think alike. It requires that we listen well, speak with love, and remain committed to the good of the whole. Disagreement is not the enemy of church health. Disconnection is. And boards that can model courageous, respectful engagement help shape a congregation capable of deeper faithfulness.

When leadership avoids difficult conversations, the consequences are subtle but real: decisions stall, trust erodes, and underground tensions grow. But when leaders stay at the table—honestly, humbly, and prayerfully—they sharpen one another, just as scripture teaches.

The Gift of Faithful Disagreement

Not all conflict is unhealthy. In fact, the Church has always included differing voices. The early Church debated theology, leadership, mission strategy—even food practices. What held them together was not perfect agreement, but shared commitment to Christ and to each other.

Boards that expect agreement on every issue may mistake silence for unity. True unity is not forged in agreement—it is forged in the fire of mutual discernment.

Faithful disagreement includes:

- **Listening without defensiveness**
- **Naming assumptions and biases**
- **Holding space for diverse experiences**

- Returning again and again to the question: What is God asking of us?

One board member once shared, "It wasn't until I stopped trying to win the argument that I realized we were all trying to serve the same mission." That moment of humility shifted the tone of the entire meeting.

Spiritual leadership does not mean avoiding discomfort. It means walking through discomfort together with courage and care.

When Conflict Becomes Harm

Not every disagreement is healthy. There are times when one or more individuals push beyond disagreement into patterns that harm the body. These are not simply strong personalities or passionate voices—they are behaviors that disrupt mission, sow division, and create spiritual exhaustion.

As outlined in the Church Bullies training, these patterns often include:

- **Persistent suspicion of others' motives**
- **Refusal to listen or engage with differing views**
- **A lack of personal accountability**
- **Obstruction of decision-making processes**
- **Regular blaming of others and discrediting of leadership**
- **Attempts to dominate or control others through fear, manipulation, or aggression**

These patterns do not serve Christ's body. When tolerated, they damage the church's witness and erode the spiritual health of the congregation.

Boards must be able to discern the difference between **prophetic challenge**, which the church must welcome, and **bullying behavior**, which the church must confront.

The courage to name these dynamics—and to respond in love but with clarity—is one of the most critical responsibilities of spiritual leadership.

Understanding How Power Operates

Church bullies rarely seize power overnight. Their influence tends to grow over time, often because others unintentionally give it to them. Sometimes it's out of fear. Other times, it's out of exhaustion. Most often, it's because leaders hope that ignoring the behavior will make it stop.

But as the *Church Bullies* training reminds us, power in the church is not something bullies are granted by God—it is often something they take, and the community allows.

Boards must reclaim their rightful role as stewards of the church's spiritual and organizational health. That includes recognizing when power has shifted away from mission and toward manipulation.

Ask:

- Who gets listened to the most in this congregation—and why?
- Are there people whose voices are avoided because of fear or past backlash?
- Do we make decisions from a place of discernment—or from a desire to avoid conflict?

Legal authority in the church resides with the board. But spiritual authority must be exercised with wisdom and care. When bullies disrupt the mission, it is not "unspiritual" to address it. It is a holy act of protection for the community God has entrusted to your care.

Establishing Healthy Boundaries

Setting boundaries is not about punishment. It is about **protecting what is sacred**.

Healthy boards establish clear expectations for behavior—both within leadership and in the congregation. These expectations are not implied. They are stated, shared, and modeled. In congregations that have endured harm, simply clarifying what respectful engagement looks like can shift the culture.

Some examples include:

- A **board covenant** that names how members will engage with one another
- A **congregational covenant** outlining how members will speak, listen, and participate
- Clear procedures for **addressing disruptive behavior**, applied consistently and compassionately

Even small churches with no formal HR policies can establish these standards. A simple handout reviewed each year. A moment of prayerful recommitment at the start of each board term. What matters is consistency—and the conviction that how we treat one another matters as much as what we believe.

Boundaries are not unloving. They are what make love sustainable in community.

Leading Through Conflict with Integrity

When boards encounter disruptive behavior or chronic conflict, their response must be rooted in clarity, humility, and unwavering commitment to God's calling. The goal is never to silence disagreement. The goal is to **protect the spiritual integrity** of the community so that it can move faithfully into its mission.

Responding with integrity includes:

- **Privately addressing the behavior early**, before it becomes a public crisis
- **Being clear about the impact**, not just the intent, of harmful words or actions
- **Using restorative practices when possible**, such as mediated conversation or spiritual guidance
- **Setting firm limits when necessary**, including limiting leadership eligibility for those engaging in repeated harm
- **Remaining grounded in prayer**, not personality

One governing board, faced with a long-standing member who regularly disrupted meetings, decided to meet with him privately. They named the behavior gently but clearly. They invited him into a process of mutual accountability. And they explained that while his passion for the church was clear, the way it was being expressed was damaging the very mission he loved. Over time, the dynamic changed. He didn't leave. But he learned to listen. And the board learned to lead.

It is never easy. But peacemaking rarely is. It takes resolve, prayer, and the conviction that the body of Christ is worth protecting.

Shaping a Culture of Growth

Boards that learn to navigate disagreement and resist bullying do more than resolve problems—they shape culture.

A culture shaped by spiritual maturity includes:

- **Openness to feedback**, without defensiveness
- **Courageous conversations**, grounded in prayer and purpose
- **Respect for diverse gifts**, even when those gifts are expressed differently
- **Resilience**, when challenges arise
- **A shared understanding that growth includes discomfort**

In such a culture, people don't have to be perfect to lead—they have to be accountable. Leaders don't have to agree on everything—they have to stay in conversation. And the mission of the church is not held hostage by any one person's control—it is shared, guided, and sustained by the Spirit.

This is what it means for iron to sharpen iron. Not to wound. But to refine.

The governing body sets the tone. When it leads with both courage and care, the congregation becomes a place where differences are not feared—but faithfully navigated.

❦ Discernment Questions

- Where are we avoiding hard conversations out of fear?
- Have we allowed harmful behaviors to persist in the name of "keeping the peace"?
- What structures or agreements could help us navigate conflict more faithfully?
- How can we ensure that disagreement sharpens us rather than divides us?
- Are we modeling the kind of spiritual maturity we hope to see in the congregation?

Chapter 26
When the Eye Rejects the Hand

Understanding power struggles, church bullies, and the spiritual cost of disconnection

"The eye cannot say to the hand, 'I have no need of you,' nor again the head to the feet, 'I have no need of you.' On the contrary, the members of the body that seem to be weaker are indispensable... If one member suffers, all suffer together with it; if one member is honored, all rejoice together with it."
-1 Corinthians 12:21–26

The body of Christ is a living system—interconnected, interdependent, and animated by love. Every part matters. Every person belongs. And yet, too often in congregational life, we see something different: tension between ministries, resentment between generations, suspicion between leadership and laity. When these divides grow, something sacred is at risk.

Paul's vision of the Church as a body calls us to unity with integrity—not a bland sameness, but a rich interweaving of gifts, perspectives, and functions. The hand is not the eye. The teacher is not the singer. The treasurer is not the deacon. But all are needed. And when one is diminished, dismissed, or disconnected, the body suffers.

The role of the governing board is to **notice these disconnections**, name them with care, and cultivate a culture where every gift is welcomed and every member is honored. This requires courage, clarity, and compassion—especially when power struggles or patterns of exclusion arise.

When Power Distorts the Body

Power is not inherently evil. In the body of Christ, power is meant to be shared, stewarded, and surrendered in service to the whole. But when power is hoarded, misused, or wielded as a tool of exclusion, it becomes toxic. Disconnection follows. And disconnection is a spiritual crisis.

This distortion often begins subtly:

- A board makes decisions without consulting ministry leaders.
- A long-serving member assumes authority without accountability.
- A single voice dominates meetings, making others feel unnecessary or unwelcome.
- A staff person withholds information, believing no one else will "do it right."

- A new volunteer offers a gift—and is told, "We don't do it that way here."

In each of these moments, the eye has rejected the hand.

And the body suffers.

A church in the Southwest learned this firsthand when its worship committee dismissed a group of young musicians eager to help lead Sunday services. "It's too different from what we're used to," one elder said. Months later, those musicians left—not just the committee, but the church. Years later, the congregation is still trying to rebuild its connection with younger adults.

These aren't personality issues. They are spiritual fractures. The board's role is not to take sides—it is to **reweave the fabric** of belonging, so that all parts of the body can serve and flourish.

Recognizing the Signs of Disconnection

Not all rejection is vocal. Often, it shows up as silence or absence. Boards must learn to recognize the subtle signs that someone—or some part of the church—is feeling unseen, undervalued, or pushed aside.

Warning signs include:

- Drop-off in participation by a specific group (young adults, elders, longtime members, etc.)
- One or two voices consistently dominating conversation
- Dismissive humor or sarcasm toward particular people or ministries
- A rise in "us vs. them" language between committees, leadership, or generations
- Resistance to feedback from outside the traditional circle of decision-makers

Boards that pay attention to who isn't speaking, who isn't present, and who isn't being heard are practicing spiritual leadership. It is easier to focus on what is loud—but healing comes when we attend to what is quiet.

The Spiritual Cost of Exclusion

When members of the body feel unnecessary, the church loses more than their participation. It loses their wisdom. Their creativity. Their passion. Their presence. Over time, a congregation may appear functional on the outside while slowly hollowing out on the inside.

Disconnection leads to disengagement. Disengagement leads to decline—not only in numbers, but in vitality.

And the pain isn't just organizational. It's personal. To be told, implicitly or explicitly, "We don't need you," wounds the spirit. It undermines the very message of the Gospel—that all are beloved, all are gifted, and all are called.

Boards must be fierce in protecting this sacred truth: **There is no unnecessary part of the body.** When someone feels pushed out, even unintentionally, the board must act.

This doesn't mean tolerating dysfunction or excusing harmful behavior. It means committing to the hard, ongoing work of **making room**, especially for those whose gifts, perspectives, or styles may be unfamiliar.

One board member described it this way: "We thought unity meant everyone doing things the same way. But real unity came when we learned to listen for God in each other's differences."

Healing the Body Through Honor

Paul's words are clear: "The members of the body that seem to be weaker are indispensable." This is not a sentimental statement. It is a strategy for renewal.

Churches that honor every member—especially the quiet ones, the newer ones, the ones who've been overlooked—are the churches where Spirit-led transformation is possible.

Boards that lead this way:

- Make intentional space for **new voices** in decision-making
- Regularly ask, **"Who else needs to be at this table?"**
- Publicly recognize **hidden contributions**, not just public leadership
- Create opportunities for **intergenerational and intercultural relationship-building**
- Model humility by **listening more than speaking**

This is not about affirmation for its own sake. It is about living into the truth that every part of the body is necessary, valued, and beloved.

When boards shift from managing conflict to honoring connection, something powerful begins to unfold. Ministries blossom. Trust deepens. The church becomes a place not just of participation—but of purpose.

Discernment Questions

- Where in our church might someone feel like "the eye has rejected the hand"?
- What voices, gifts, or groups have we unintentionally excluded from leadership or decision-making?
- Are there any patterns of dominance, silence, or disconnection we've come to accept as normal?
- How can we become more intentional about honoring every part of the body?
- What does it look like for us to truly believe that all are indispensable in the body of Christ?

Chapter 27
Unity in Calling

Becoming one body, rooted in God's purpose, faithful to the work before us

"There is one body and one Spirit, just as you were called to the one hope of your calling… one Lord, one faith, one baptism, one God and Father of all, who is above all and through all and in all."
– Ephesians 4:4–6

The Church is not just an organization. It is not simply a gathering place. It is a people—**called together by God**, shaped by the Spirit, and sent into the world with purpose.

When we forget that calling, we drift. We busy ourselves with tasks. We become managers of maintenance rather than stewards of mission. But when we remember—truly remember—that we are a body formed and sent by God, everything changes.

We listen differently. We lead differently. We love differently.

This is the call of governance: to keep the flame of that calling alive. Not by clinging to what has been, but by discerning what is now. Not by enforcing unity, but by inviting participation in something greater than ourselves. When we lead this way, something holy happens.

We become the Church again.

Called Together, Not Just Gathered

Churches do not exist by accident. Every congregation—whether in a small town or urban center, whether 30 members or 3,000—exists because the Spirit has planted something there. A seed of grace. A word of hope. A mission for this time and this place.

Governance is not about keeping the institution alive. It is about keeping that seed nourished. Boards are not managers of religious programming. They are **stewards of the call**.

This calling is not generic. It is specific. What God asks of one congregation may be entirely different than another. The call may change over time. But it always begins with listening.

When a governing body discerns God's unique call for their church, they find their true center. The budget begins to make sense. The building becomes a tool, not a burden. Meetings find purpose. Tensions ease—not because everyone agrees, but because everyone is pulling in the same direction.

One board member described it this way: "Once we named our calling, we stopped fighting about what we should do—and started asking how to do it together."

That is unity. Not uniformity. Not control. **Shared commitment to what God is doing in and through us.**

The Power of Alignment

Throughout this book, we have explored what it means to align energy and resources with God's calling. But alignment is not just about efficient operations or better communication. It is a **spiritual discipline**.

When a church aligns its structures, its finances, and its leadership with its divine purpose, something greater than strategy unfolds. The Spirit begins to move freely. Ministries flourish. Leaders are renewed. The congregation rediscovers joy—not from busyness, but from clarity.

Alignment creates integrity. Integrity generates trust. And trust invites participation.

This is how congregations grow—not just in size, but in **spiritual depth**.

It is why governance matters.

Not because we love meetings. But because **we love the Church enough to build the vessel that can carry the Spirit's work.**

One Body, Many Gifts—One Purpose

The metaphor of the body, used by Paul and echoed throughout the Christian tradition, reminds us that unity is not found in sameness. It is found in shared purpose.

In every congregation, the Spirit distributes gifts—some visible, some quiet. Administration. Wisdom. Mercy. Encouragement. Prophecy. Vision. Hospitality. Finance. Prayer. Each of these is sacred. Each is needed.

The role of governance is not to elevate some gifts above others. It is to create the space where all gifts can be offered, honored, and woven into the whole.

This kind of unity cannot be mandated. It must be **cultivated**:

- Through structures that invite shared leadership
- Through processes that honor different voices
- Through a culture that says, "You are needed here. You are called here."

When this happens, the church becomes not a place people go, but a **people on a journey together**. That journey is animated by the Spirit, guided by discernment, and empowered by love.

The Witness of a United Church

In a fractured world, a united church becomes a powerful witness. Not a church that avoids conflict—but one that moves through it faithfully. Not a church without questions—but one grounded in its call. Not a church obsessed with its own survival—but one committed to the flourishing of the world around it.

This is the church the world is hungry to see.

A church that feeds the poor with joy.
A church that welcomes the outsider with humility.
A church that stewards its resources with faithfulness.
A church that makes decisions in prayer.

A church that listens more than it speaks.
A church that leads—not because it has all the answers—but because it is willing to follow the Spirit together.

This is the church governance can make possible.

And this is the kind of governance this book has called you into— not governance as bureaucracy, but as **a form of discipleship**.

Not a duty, but a calling.
Not a burden, but a blessing.
Not a task, but a testimony.

❦ Discernment Questions

- What is the unique calling God has placed on our congregation in this time and place?
- In what ways are our governance, finances, and ministries aligned—or misaligned—with that calling?
- Are we inviting every part of the body to participate fully in the work God has given us?
- What spiritual practices can help us remain rooted in our call as a governing body?
- How might our unity in calling become a witness to our community and a blessing to the world?

Conclusion: Embracing the Call

"This is the way; walk in it."
— Isaiah 30:21

The pages of this book are filled with structures, questions, and strategies — but they were never the destination. They were meant only as tools. The true goal was always this: that your church, in this season, might listen well and live faithfully into God's calling.

We believe that governance is a ministry. A sacred trust. An act of love. And when it is carried out with care, courage, and clarity, it has the power to bind us together in purpose and peace.

You, dear leader, are part of something holy. Whether you serve for a season or a lifetime, your willingness to lead is a gift to the Body of Christ. Thank you for offering your energy, your wisdom, and your presence to the work of discernment and stewardship.

There will be moments when you're unsure. When the way forward seems unclear. Pause. Breathe. Return to the Spirit. Return to the call. Remember that you are not alone. The God who called you is faithful.

And now — may you go forth not with all the answers, but with hearts attuned to the One who speaks. May your governance be marked by grace. May your decisions reflect discernment. And may your community find joy in walking together, united in calling.

Appendix

Tools for Spirit-Led Governance

This appendix includes a glossary of essential terms and a practical checklist to support Spirit-led governance. Additional templates and sample policies referenced throughout the book — including the Gift Acceptance Policy, Board Covenant, and financial planning tools — are available in the Resource Library of the Effective Church Leadership Community. Access is free with the QR code or web link provided at the beginning of the book.

Glossary of Governance & Finance Terms

Bylaws: The official governing rules of the church that define leadership structures, voting, meetings, and procedural guidelines.

Calling: The unique purpose or direction God is asking a church to follow in a specific season.

Designated Funds: Contributions given for a specific purpose, by donor request, honored by board agreement.

Discernment: A spiritual process of listening for God's guidance, especially in decision-making, often through prayer and group reflection.

Endowment: A long-term fund held by a church or nonprofit, where the principal is invested and earnings may be used for ministry.

Fiduciary Responsibility: The legal and ethical obligation of board members to act in the best interest of the organization and its mission.

GAAP: 'Generally Accepted Accounting Principles,' a standardized framework for financial reporting and transparency.

Restricted Funds: Contributions with legal obligations for their use, based on donor instructions that must be followed.

Undesignated Funds: Contributions made without a specific purpose, available for use at the board's discretion.

UPMIFA: The Uniform Prudent Management of Institutional Funds Act — the legal standard guiding the investment and use of charitable endowments.

10 Practices of Spirit-Led Governance

1. Begin decisions with prayer and listening.

2. Align policies with Calling—not just precedent.

3. Use financial reports to tell the story of ministry.

4. Balance strategic planning with spiritual discernment.

5. Clarify board roles to prevent burnout and confusion.

6. Make space for silence and reflection in meetings.

7. Respond to conflict with grace, clarity, and care.

8. Review and revise bylaws every 3–5 years.

9. Discern alignment before launching new initiatives.

10. End each meeting by naming where God's presence was sensed.

Scripture Index by Chapter

Chapter 1: The Spirit Has Placed Us Here
1 Corinthians 12:18

Chapter 2: Paths Made Straight
Proverbs 3:5–6

Chapter 3: The Threefold Cord
Ecclesiastes 4:12

Matthew 18:20

Colossians 3:14

Chapter 4: Stewarding the Storehouse
1 Peter 4:10

Chapter 5: Until the Sun Set
Exodus 17:12

Chapter 6: Hearing the Silence
1 Kings 19:11–12

Chapter 7: Wisdom That Builds the House
Habakkuk 2:2

Proverbs 24:3–4

Chapter 8: Forming Our Structure
Titus 1:5

Exodus 18:21-23

Chapter 9: Sealed in Covenant
Nehemiah 9:38

Chapter 10: Meeting in the Presence of God
Habakkuk 2:1

1 Samuel 3:10

Psalm 46:10

Chapter 11: Movement Leads to Stillness
1 Thessalonians 5:21

Chapter 12: Shepherds After My Own Heart
Jeremiah 3:15

Ezekiel 33:7

Matthew 10:16

Acts 20:28-30

Chapter 13: Protected by Purpose
2 Corinthians 8:21

Chapter 14: Keeping the Wolves at Bay
Romans 13:1

Titus 3:1-2

1 Peter 2:13

Chapter 15: Plans Committed in Prayer
Proverbs 16:3

Chapter 16: Written on Our Hearts
2 Corinthians 3:2–3

Chapter 17: Bringing in the Harvest
Luke 14:23

Galatians 6:9

Matthew 9:37–38

Chapter 18: Leaving an Inheritance
Proverbs 13:22

Chapter 19: Threads to Refuse
Genesis 14:22–23

Chapter 20: Beyond Our Capacity
2 Corinthians 12:9

Chapter 21: Blessed Are the Peacemakers
Matthew 5:9

Chapter 22: Healed and Whole Again
Isaiah 58:12

Chapter 23: When the Spirit Says No
Proverbs 27:17

Ephesians 4:15

Chapter 24: Unity in Calling
1 Corinthians 12:21–26

Ephesians 4:4–6

Effective Church Leadership Community

Equipping Leaders to Serve Faithfully, Lead Boldly, and Follow the Spirit Together

Leadership in the church is sacred, courageous work. You don't have to do it alone.

The Effective Church Leadership Community is a free online space for pastors, treasurers, board members, and ministry leaders to connect, grow, and lead with clarity. Through webinars, tools, best practices, and supportive conversation, we help churches align energy and resources with God's calling — not alone, but together.

Whether you're stepping into leadership or guiding others, this community offers practical wisdom and spiritual encouragement for the road ahead.

Scan to join or visit the link below:

https://community.churchtrainingcenter.com/plans/1529909

Continue the Journey

Your leadership journey doesn't end here. Whether you're just beginning or seeking to go deeper, these resources are available to support you and your church as you grow in faithfulness, clarity, and confidence.

Serving the Call
A Training Manual for New Governance Body Members
Forming Faithful Leaders for Sacred Responsibility.

A companion guide that equips church board members with the tools and spiritual grounding to serve with integrity, clarity, and confidence. Available in the Effective Church Leadership Community.

Called Together

A Spirit-Led Discernment Guide for Congregational Planning

Keith Clark-Hoyos
Founder, Church Training Center

Called Together
A Spirit-Led Discernment Guide for Congregational Planning

This reflective, prayer-centered planning tool helps congregations discern God's calling, align energy and resources, and move forward in unity. Designed for retreats, seasons of listening, or transition periods.

Let's Keep Going

If this book has sparked clarity, raised questions, or left you longing for more support, we're here to help.

Church Training Center offers coaching, training, and consulting for church boards, pastors, and leaders who want to align faithfully with God's call — and sustain the journey over time.

To explore next steps or schedule a consultation, visit:

www.ChurchTrainingCenter.com

Or reach out directly at:
service@ChurchTrainingCenter.com

Leadership Rooted in Discernment.
Governance guided by God's call.

Church boards and leaders carry a sacred responsibility — to listen deeply, act faithfully, and steward the mission God has entrusted to their congregation.

Embracing Our Call is a practical and Spirit-centered guide for governing body members who want to lead with integrity, clarity, and purpose. Whether you're new to leadership or renewing your structure, this book offers:

- A Spirit-led model for aligning Calling, Energy, and Resources
- Guidance for board roles, bylaws, and faithful decision-making
- Practical tools for financial planning and accountability
- Reflection prompts and scriptures for communal discernment

Written with warmth, wisdom, and real-world experience, this book is more than a manual — it's an invitation to lead as a unified body, walking together in faith.

"This is a Spirit-centered resource that reminds us that discernment is not a one-time event, but an ongoing practice. A timely and powerful tool for any church seeking clarity and direction."
— Rev. Doug Zimmerman, Treasurer, St. John UCC

Keith Clark-Hoyos is a coach, consultant, and spiritual leader who helps churches align structure and Spirit. He brings decades of experience in judicatory leadership, nonprofit consulting, and Daoist contemplative practice. He is the founder of Church Training Center.

Learn more or join our community at **www.ChurchTrainingCenter.com**

www.ingramcontent.com/pod-product-compliance
Lightning Source LLC
Chambersburg PA
CBHW022001160426
43197CB00007B/217